BrightRED Study Guide

Curriculum for Excellence

N5

PHYSICAL EDUCATION

Susan McGrenaghan and Lewis Porteous

BrightRED
PUBLISHING

First published in 2014 by:
Bright Red Publishing Ltd
1 Torphichen Street
Edinburgh
EH3 8HX

A CIP record for this book is available from the British Library

ISBN 978-1-906736-43-9

With thanks to:
PDQ Digital Media Solutions Ltd (layout) and Sue Moody, Bright Writing (edit)

Cover design and series book design by Caleb Rutherford – e i d e t i c

Acknowledgements
Every effort has been made to seek all copyright holders. If any have been overlooked, then Bright Red Publishing will be delighted to make the necessary arrangements.

Permission has been sought from all relevant copyright holders and Bright Red Publishing are grateful for the use of the following:
Jon Candy (CC BY-SA 2.0)[1] (p 6); Stano Novak (CC BY 2.5)[2] (p 7); 3 photos from IvanWalsh.com (CC BY 2.0)[3] (p 7); Ami Parikh/Shutterstock.com (p 9); © Marie-Lan Nguyen/Wikimedia Commons (CC-BY 3.0)[4] (p 10); Pierre-Yves Beaudouin/ Wikimedia Commons (CC-BY-SA-4.0)[5] (p 10); Joel Solomon (CC BY 2.0)[3] (p 10); roanokecollege (CC BY 2.0)[3] (p 10); 金娜 Kim S (CC BY-SA 2.0)[1] (p 10); eelke dekker (CC BY 2.0)[3] (p 13); Mike Kalasnik (CC BY-SA 2.0)[1] (p 14); Richard Smith (CC BY 2.0)[3] (p 15); fourthandfifteen (CC BY 2.0)[3] (p 15); Denis Kuvaev/Shutterstock.com (p 15); Bauken77 (CC BY-SA 3.0)[6] (p 17); palmipode (CC BY 2.0)[3] (p 17); Doha Stadium Plus Qatar (CC BY 2.0)[3] (p 17); Pavel L Photo and Video/Shutterstock.com (p 19); Raphael Goetter (CC BY 2.0)[3] (p 21); G.Garitan (CC BY-SA 3.0)[6] (p 21); Thiago Piccoli (CC BY 2.0)[3] (p 21); Bidgee (CC BY-SA 3.0 AU)[7] (p 22); David W. Leindecker/shutterstock.com (p 22); Royal New Zealand Navy (CC BY-ND 2.0)[8] (p 27); 2 photos from istolethetv (CC BY 2.0)[3] (p 28); Yu Morita (CC BY-SA 2.0)[1] (p 29); nazreth/freeimages.com (p 29); Baum332 (CC BY-SA 3.0)[6] (p 41); Photographer's Mate 2nd Class Terry Spain (public domain) (p 43); Aringo (CC BY-SA 2.0)[1] (p 44); Erik van Leeuwen (CC BY-SA 3.0)[6] (p 45); Bill (CC BY 2.0)[3] (p 45); lightpoet/Shutterstock.com (p 46); makieni/Shutterstock.com (p 47); Fanny Schertzer (CC BY-SA 3.0)[6] (p 47); Paul Rowlett (CC BY 2.0)[3] (p 50); cdephotos (CC BY 2.0)[3] (p 53); PierreSelim (CC BY-SA 3.0)[6] (p 54); GalianoIsland (CC BY-SA 3.0)[6] (p 55); Zorro2212 (CC BY-SA 3.0)[6] (p 56); Selma Bears (CC BY 2.0)[3] (p 56); Iryna Melnyk/Shutterstock.com (p 58); James Gathany (public domain) (p 59); Sarah Connors (CC BY 2.0)[3] (p 59); U.S. Navy photo by Photographer's Mate 1st Class Brien Aho (public domain) (p 60); Gayvoronskaya_Yana/Shutterstock.com (p 61); Africa Studio/Shutterstock.com (p 61); bonchan/Shutterstock.com (p 61); Robyn Mackenzie/Shutterstock.com (p 61); Tom Page (CC BY-SA 2.0)[1] (p 62); kance (CC BY 2.0)[3] (p 63); Chief Photographer's Mate Chris Desmond (public domain) (p 64); isafmedia (CC BY 2.0)[3] (p 66); Tab59 (CC BY-SA 2.0)[1] (p 67); Boss Tweed (CC BY 2.0)[3] (p 68); Deklofenak/shutterstock.com (p 68); rdcock/freeimages.com (p 70); Tristan Haskins (CC BY-SA 3.0)[6] (p 70); Doha Stadium Plus Qatar (CC BY 2.0)[3] (p 72); Photographer's Mate 2nd Class Damon J. Moritz (public domain) (p 72); Bryan Allison (CC BY-SA 2.0)[1] (p 73); Carine06 (CC BY-SA 2.0)[1] (p 74); Carine06 (CC BY-SA 2.0)[1] (p 75); © Christopher Lofthouse (p 76); Wilson Dias/Abr (CC BY 3.0 BR) (p 76); Simply Swim UK (CC BY-SA 2.0)[1] (p 77); Land Rover MENA (CC BY 2.0)[3] (p 80); sainthorant Daniel/shutterstock.com (p82); Lilyana Vynogradova/shutterstock.com (p83); Windsor Tennis Club Belfast (CC BY 2.0)[3] (p84); Ronnie Macdonald (CC BY 2.0)[3] (p84); dotshock/shutterstock.com (p85); Bruce Tuten (CC BY 2.0)[3] (p85).

(CC BY-SA 2.0)[1]	http://creativecommons.org/licenses/by-sa/2.0/
(CC BY 2.5)[2]	http://creativecommons.org/licenses/by/2.5/
(CC BY 2.0)[3]	http://creativecommons.org/licenses/by/2.0/
(CC-BY 3.0)[4]	http://creativecommons.org/licenses/by/3.0/
(CC-BY-SA-4.0)[5]	https://creativecommons.org/licenses/by-sa/4.0/
(CC BY-SA 3.0)[6]	http://creativecommons.org/licenses/by-sa/3.0/
(CC BY-SA 3.0 AU)[7]	https://creativecommons.org/licenses/by-sa/3.0/au/
(CC BY-ND 2.0)[8]	http://creativecommons.org/licenses/by-nd/2.0/

Printed and bound in the UK by Martins the Printers.

CONTENTS LIST

INTRODUCING NATIONAL 5 PHYSICAL EDUCATION

The National 5 Physical Education course will enable you to develop and demonstrate a comprehensive range of movement and performance skills in physical activities through practical and experiential learning. You will also develop an increased understanding of the important link between fitness and good health.

The course content will help you to develop knowledge and understanding of the different factors that impact on performance through investigating, analysing, developing and evaluating your own performance.

The National 5 Physical Education course comprises two units and a course assessment.

To gain the full award at National 5, you will need to pass both units and their outcomes, and the course assessment. The outcomes are graded on a pass/fail basis.

PHYSICAL EDUCATION: PERFORMANCE SKILLS (NATIONAL 5) UNIT

To pass this unit, you have to meet the requirements of the following outcome:

Outcome 1

Demonstrate a comprehensive range of movement and performance skills in physical activities.
To meet this outcome, you must:
- Demonstrate straightforward performance skills and movements, as well as some more complex actions, with **consistency** in a fluent, controlled manner.
- Show body and spatial awareness with **rhythms** and patterns.
- Work productively with others.
- Effectively and safely use straightforward techniques and compositions or **tactics**.
- Respond to a variety of events with appropriate decisions and straightforward adaptations.

PHYSICAL EDUCATION: FACTORS IMPACTING ON PERFORMANCE (NATIONAL 5) UNIT

To pass this unit, you have to meet the requirements of the following three outcomes:

Outcome 1

Demonstrate knowledge and understanding of factors that impact on performance in physical activities.
To meet this outcome, you must:
- Explain methods you used to identify factors that impacted on your performance.
- Explain the impact of positive and negative factors on your performance.
- Identify approaches you can use to develop your performance, and explain why these approaches are appropriate.

Outcome 2

Develop personal performance in physical activities.
To meet this outcome, you must:
- Describe your strengths and areas you need to develop to improve your performance.
- Prepare and implement a personal development plan (pdp) that focuses on clear development targets.
- Select and apply approaches to improve your performance.
- Monitor and record your personal development sessions to ensure ongoing progress.

Outcome 3

Evaluate the performance development process.
To meet this outcome, you must:
- Seek varying forms of feedback.

contd

- Evaluate the effectiveness of your pdp in supporting your performance development.
- Re-gather information on your performance to evaluate progress.
- Identify future developmental needs to continue improving whole performance.

COURSE ASSESSMENT

The National 5 Physical Education Course assessment has two components:
- Performance
- Portfolio

Component 1 – performance

The performance component is graded internally within your centre, school or college.

The performance component is worth 60 marks. The marks contribute to 60% of your overall marks for the course assessment. The course will be graded A–D.

The performance will be graded on a single performance, the context of which must be challenging, competitive and/or demanding. You are expected to plan and prepare for, perform and evaluate this single performance.

The performance has three sections:
- Section 1 – Planning and preparation (10 marks)
- Section 2 – Performance (40 marks)
- Section 3 – Evaluation (10 marks)

Section 1 – Planning and preparation will include assessment of the following:
- Consideration of any challenges you might face during your performance.
- Your ability to prepare mentally, physically and technically to meet these challenges before your performance – for example, mental rehearsal, warm up or pre-match habits that help you to focus
- The structural, strategic, tactical or compositional decisions you make before your performance to overcome these challenges – for example, performing to your (and your team's) strengths, to the conditions on the day of the performance or to the strengths and weaknesses of the opposition. See pp82–4 for more on this.

Section 2 – Performance will include assessment of the following:
- Your demonstration of performance repertoire.
- **Control** and fluency of your movement and performance skills.
- Your **decision-making** throughout your performance.
- The effectiveness of following through on decision-making.
- The extent to which you follow rules and regulations and display **etiquette**.
- How well you control your emotions.

Section 3 – Evaluation will include assessment of the following:
- Your reflection on the performance and how it relates to your planning and preparation.
- Your justification of any structural, strategic, tactical or compositional adaptations that you made during the game.
- Your evaluation of your overall performance. See p85 for more on this.

Component 2 – portfolio

The portfolio component is graded externally, by the SQA.

The portfolio component is worth 40 marks. The marks contribute to 40% of the overall marks for the course assessment. The course will be graded A–D.

This portfolio has three sections:
- Section 1 – Understanding factors that impact on performance (8 marks)
- Section 2 – Planning, developing and implementing approaches to enhance personal performance (16 marks)
- Section 3 – Monitoring, recording and evaluating performance development (16 marks). See pp86–91 for more.

HOW THIS STUDY GUIDE WILL HELP YOU

This Study Guide (supported by the Bright Red Digital Zone) will provide the knowledge and tools to pass the four outcomes and prepare you for the internal and external assessments.

Helpful hints are provided in the 'Don't forget' sections and there are video links for practical examples. The 'Things to do and think about' at the end of each page and online tests will get you thinking and test your knowledge of each section.

PERFORMANCE

PLANNING AND PREPARING FOR PERFORMANCE 1

INTRODUCTION

The performance component of the course assessment is a major area of the course: it makes up 60% of your final grade. It is therefore important that you not only know and understand how to develop your own performance, but that you are also able to put this knowledge and understanding into practice in a more pressurised setting. For your practical assessment you will be required to do the following:

- Plan and prepare for your performance
- Perform
- Evaluate your performance

To help you achieve the best mark possible in the performance component there are a number of areas included in this chapter that will provide you with knowledge and understanding about the following:

* Planning and preparing for performance
* The nature and demands of activities
* Characteristics of a skilled performance
* Classification of skills
* Aspects of fitness impacting on performance
* Feedback

PLANNING AND PREPARING: PHYSICAL, TECHNICAL AND MENTAL WARM-UP

Planning and preparing for a performance is important to ensure you are physically, technically and mentally ready to perform to the highest level you possibly can. As well as this, you need to ensure that you (and your team) have selected the correct tactics, structures, strategies or compositions to enable you to play to your strengths.

Physical warm-up

Physical warm-ups can take many forms, and depend on the nature and demands of the activity. Most physical warm-ups start with a form of light aerobic exercise – for example, jogging, cycling, rowing or swimming. Once an aerobic warm-up has been carried out, athletes usually carry out a series of stretches. Stretching can either be done on the move (dynamic) or standing still (static).

Dynamic stretching is particularly popular among athletes as the movements are done on the move and can be adapted to mirror movements similar to those which the athlete is about to perform.

Technical warm-up

Technical warm-ups are designed to focus on the specific skills that the athlete is about to use in their chosen activity. During a technical warm-up, athletes will take part in practices or drills that help remind the body of specific movements and movement patterns.

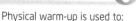

EXAMPLE FOOTBALL

Footballers usually take part in a technical warm-up before a match. This technical warm-up might focus on giving and receiving passes to develop their 'touch' before a game.

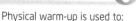

contd

> **EXAMPLE**   DANCE
>
> Before a competition, dancers practise isolated movements to prepare their bodies for the type of movements they will be using during their routine.

Mental warm-up

A mental warm-up can serve many purposes for an athlete. Prior to a performance an athlete needs to:

- raise their **level of arousal** (motivate themselves)
- lower their level of arousal (calm themselves down)
- focus on their whole performance or certain parts of it
- mentally rehearse a specific routine.

Different approaches suit different individuals. The table below outlines some examples of the methods athletes use to mentally warm-up. (You might be able to think of more yourself.)

METHOD	EFFECT
Listening to music	This can either be used to calm an athlete down before a performance if they are nervous, or to raise **motivation** levels.
Mental rehearsal	Athletes often imagine performing certain skills to focus their mind on the task they are about to perform. This can involve a single movement or a series of movements linked together.
Set routine	Athletes might have a routine they carry out prior to every performance. This can range from carrying out specific actions before performing a skill, to eating the same food before every performance. The goal of a routine is to focus the mind on the task in hand.
Positive self-talk	Positive self-talk is used to raise an athlete's self-confidence. Prior to a performance, an athlete can use positive self-talk to ensure that there are no negative thoughts or doubts in their mind.
Team talk	Prior to a performance, it is common for a coach or manager to speak to an athlete or team. Team talks are designed to focus the player or players and to motivate them to perform to the best of their ability.
Breathing techniques	An athlete might use breathing techniques to reduce anxiety levels by regulating their heart rate and counteracting the negative effects of adrenaline.

VIDEO LINK

Head to www.brightredbooks.net/N5PE and watch Jonny Wilkinson demonstrate his pre-kicking routine.

THINGS TO DO AND THINK ABOUT

Think about sports you have watched on TV. Can you list examples of set **routines** that professional sports people have?

ONLINE TEST

Take the 'Planning and preparing for performance' test at www.brightredbooks.net/N5PE

PLANNING AND PREPARING FOR PERFORMANCE 2

AN EXAMPLE OF A WARM-UP

EXAMPLE   RUGBY WARM-UP

Here is an example of a warm-up a rugby player might go through prior to a game.

WHEN	PHYSICAL	TECHNICAL	MENTAL
1 hour before game `01:00:00`			Player has eaten a good meal before the game. Player listens to music on their way. Player changes into kit.
50 minutes before game `00:50:00`	Player does light aerobic warm-up to raise heart rate and take oxygenated blood to the muscles.		
40 minutes before game `00:40:00`	Player does dynamic stretching – for example, high knees, heel flicks, press-ups, lunges and squats.		
30 minutes before game `00:30:00`		Player does technical warm-up – passing ball in lines of four, practising tackle technique on tackle bags.	
20 minutes before game `00:20:00`		Player takes part in a 'team run-through' in which the team use unopposed practice to rehearse structure.	
10 minutes before game `00:15:00`			Player returns to changing room, listens to music again and spends 5 minutes mentally rehearsing their role during the game and using positive self-talk.
5 minutes before game `00:05:00`			Coach/captain team talk outlines tactics and motivates players.

SELECTING APPROPRIATE STRUCTURE, STRATEGIES, TACTICS OR COMPOSITIONS

The structure, strategy, tactics or composition that you (and your team) choose before a performance can have a big impact on how successful your overall performance is.

For example, before a game of football a team will need to consider:

- their own strengths and areas of weakness
- availability of players
- the opponents' strengths and areas of weakness
- the opponents' structure and strategy
- environmental conditions such as the state of the pitch and weather
- the meaning of the game (for example – cup match or a match played over two legs).

On the other hand, a diver would have to consider:

- the meaning of the event (qualifying/final round)
- their own ability/skill set
- the order in which they perform their dives (that is, do they start with an easy dive and increase difficulty as the competition progresses, or start with a high-difficulty dive in the hope that they perform well first time, which will put pressure on other competitors?).

DIET

The food and drink you consume before a performance can have an impact on how you feel and perform. Eating the wrong types of food before taking part in a sport can lead to low energy levels and cause the body to become fatigued. When they are preparing for a performance, athletes tend to eat foods that are high in carbohydrates such as pasta, potatoes, rice or porridge. These types of food release energy slowly, providing the athlete with enough energy to sustain their whole performance.

ONLINE

Check out the 'NHS: Food for Sports' link at www.brightredbooks.net/N5PE for more on diet.

DON'T FORGET

Hydration is as important as diet when preparing for performance.

As well as eating the correct foods, it is important to be well hydrated before a performance. Not being properly hydrated can lead to loss of energy, cramping and eventually dehydration. Athletes should, therefore, drink plenty of water before a performance to ensure they are properly hydrated going into the competition.

ONLINE TEST

Take the 'Planning and preparing for performance' test at www.brightredbooks.net/N5PE

THINGS TO DO AND THINK ABOUT

Think about the warm-ups you do for the activities on your course, or activities you do for a club. Do you have a set warm-up? Try writing it down using a similar table to the one on p8.

NATURE AND DEMANDS OF ACTIVITIES

INDIVIDUAL AND TEAM ACTIVITIES

Within Physical Education and sport there are lots of different types of activities that we can participate in. Often these sports can be split into individual and team activities. An individual activity is one where the activity is performed by one person who is playing against an opponent – for example, as in singles tennis. A team activity involves you working as part of a group – for example, as in basketball.

However, there are variations within these definitions. For example, some individual activities can be performed by one person totally on their own – as in golf. In some team activities, the team might only consist of two people or players – as in doubles table tennis. Or the team might consist of many members – as in a football team.

COMPETITIVE AND NON-COMPETITIVE

As well as being defined as individual or team, activities can also be categorised into competitive or non-competitive. Competitive activities usually involve a **contest** between two or more rivals, with each rival trying to win.

Non-competitive activities are usually performed or played for the following reasons:

- self-satisfaction – participating for the thrill of the sport, enjoyment
- health benefits – keeping themselves fit, to relieve stress and tension (especially if they lead a hectic life)
- social aspects – meeting new people or friends.

Contests

Contests are either directly competitive or indirectly competitive.

Activities that are directly competitive mean that you have a direct bearing or influence on what your opponent does – for example, as in netball, lacrosse and hockey.

Activities that are classed as being indirectly competitive mean that your own performance does not affect the performance of your opponent(s) – for example, as in gymnastics, golf or skiing.

THE DEMANDS OF ACTIVITIES

The physical, mental, social and emotional demands that are put on individuals when they participate in sport are often dependant on the type of activity that they are participating in. Someone who is participating in a non-competitive individual activity, such as jogging, might not feel the mental pressures and strain of someone who is participating in a competitive activity.

So what are the demands that we are faced with when participating in sport?

Physical demands

The physical demands will depend on:

- how fit we are
- how demanding the activity is
- whether we are participating in the activity to benefit our health or as part of a competition.

Mental and emotional demands

The mental and emotional demands will depend on:

- whether we have to mentally prepare before participating in sport
- how well we are able to prepare mentally and whether anxiety has a positive or negative effect on our performance
- our ability to manage our emotions
- our levels of **concentration**.

Social demands

The social demands will depend on:

- whether the purpose of participating in a specific activity is to meet new friends and form new relationships
- how well we interact with other people
- whether we participate in specific sports due to our gender or stereotypes
- the initial expense of starting a new activity.

For more on this topic, refer to the 'Table of factors that impact on performance' in Appendix 1 at the end of this Study Guide.

DON'T FORGET

An individual's reasons for participating in a particular sport will vary from one person to the next. We must consider whether they want to play competitively, recreationally or socially. Do they want to play in a team or pursue more individual sports? Can they afford to travel to and from venues for training? Can they afford the correct equipment to participate? Are they influenced by stereotypical views towards some sports which prevent them from playing them?

ONLINE TEST

How well have you learned about the nature and demands of activities? Go online and test yourself at www.brightredbooks.net/N5PE

ONLINE

For more on the different reasons why people might take part in sport, follow the 'Benefits of sport' link at www.brightredbooks.net/N5PE

THINGS TO DO AND THINK ABOUT

1   List as many examples of individual and team activities as you can in the table below:

TYPE OF ACTIVITY	DESCRIPTION		EXAMPLE
Individual activity	Individual (plays totally on their own)		*Golf,*
	Individual (plays on their own against another opponent)		*Table tennis,*
Team activity	Lots of team mates		*Football,*
	2, 3 or 4 team mates		*Tennis Doubles,*

2   Think about the definitions of individual/team, non-competitive and directly/indirectly competitive activities described in this topic. Complete the table below by filling in examples and descriptions of your own.

TYPE OF ACTIVITY	EXAMPLE	DESCRIPTION
Individual (non-competitive)	Aerobics	Alone, performed for health and social benefits.
Individual (directly competitive)		
Individual (indirectly competitive)		
Team (non-competitive)		
Team (directly competitive)	Football	11 vs. 11, involving tactical strategies. Attacking and defending and vice versa.
Team (indirectly competitive)		

CHARACTERISTICS OF A SKILLED PERFORMANCE

WHAT MAKES A SKILLED PERFORMANCE?

To be able to investigate and develop your own performance, you need to be able to recognise what makes a skilled performance. Skilled performance has four characteristics:

1. The sequence of movements is carried out in a fluent, controlled way.
2. Movements are performed with maximum efficiency and minimum effort.
3. Correct options are selected and performed consistently.
4. The skill is relative to the performer's experience.

For example, your ability and experience in gymnastics will determine the type of skills and techniques you are able to incorporate efficiently into your floor routine. An Olympic-standard gymnast will have a broad range of skills they can perform during their routine. To a spectator, these skills should look fluent, controlled and executed with the minimum of effort.

SKILLED/MODEL PERFORMERS

A skilled/model performer:

- is alert and ready
- is accurate
- demonstrates high quality of movement
- demonstrates a wide repertoire of skills
- demonstrates excellent decision-making
- is agile
- can expose opponent weaknesses

- demonstrates efficient movement patterns
- knows when to execute specific skills/ techniques
- makes maximum output with minimum effort.

 VIDEO LINK

Head to www. brightredbooks.net/N5PE and watch the video of the highly skilled performers Andy Murray and Roger Federer playing a rally.

 DON'T FORGET

A 'skill' is your ability to carry out a linked sequence of movements – for example, a 'skill' in basketball = shooting. 'Technique' is a way of performing this skill – for example, 'shooting technique' in basketball = jump shot, set shot, lay-up.

EXAMPLE   TENNIS: MODEL PERFORMERS

The model performer shows movement skills that are fluent and controlled. They are relaxed and ready and their footwork is light and quick, which enables them to get into the correct position to play the selected shot and to recover to the middle of the court between shots. This is achieved using the minimal amount of energy. The model performer is also able to vary and adapt by using a range of skills and techniques. In doing so, the performer draws on knowledge from previous experience to ensure appropriate decisions are made.

PROCESSING INFORMATION WHEN LEARNING SKILLS

When learning and executing skills, you must process information in a very short period of time. As you become more competent in the activity, you will learn how to process information more quickly and effectively.

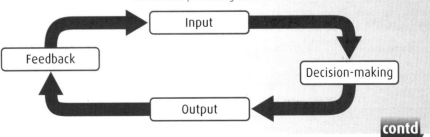

Information processing model

contd

- **Input:** this is the information you receive from your senses – for example, sight and sound.
- **Decision-making:** once you have processed this information, you must select the **relevant** data and make decisions based upon that information.
- **Output:** this is the movement sequence you choose when you have gone through the input and decision-making stages of the process.
- **Feedback:** this is the information you receive about your performance – for example, sight, sound and feel – during and after your movement sequence.

This cycle is repeated every time there is a decision to be made or a shot to be played during an activity. Experienced performers work through the process in a split second to select the correct movement pattern.

> **EXAMPLE**   TABLE TENNIS: PROCESSING INFORMATION
>
> If you watch any table tennis match you'll observe that the players constantly have to make decisions based on a variety of information:
>
> - **Input:** The players position themselves at the table, ready to respond to a variety of shots their opponent might play. Their senses have to take in information about the opponent's shot – for example, where the ball will bounce and whether they will play a backhand/forehand shot or a slice/top spin.
> - **Decision-making:** The players' brains have to separate all the essential and non-essential information that their senses have gathered, and then make a decision based upon this information.
> - **Output:** The players have to execute the correct shots and, by doing so, try to gain advantage in the rally.
> - **Feedback:** The players have to use their quality of return to evaluate their performance and plan their next shot. For example, was the type of shot they chose good enough to gain an advantage in the rally? Did the ball land on the area of the table that they were aiming for?

VIDEO LINK

Head to www. brightredbooks.net/N5PE and watch the video clip of a table tennis match. The players in this video clip are of an extremely high standard and are therefore able to make decisions and adapt their shots in a split second.

BREAKING SKILLS DOWN

One way of analysing a skilled performance is to break the skill down into three separate parts or **subroutines**. These are:

1   Preparation   2   Action   3   Recovery

Breaking skills down allows us to analyse what a performer does in the build-up to a skill, during a skill and immediately following the execution of a skill.

> **EXAMPLE**   BADMINTON: OVERHEAD CLEAR
>
> - **Preparation:** player is side on to the net with weight predominantly on their back foot. Racket is pulled back with non-racket hand 'tracking' the shuttle.
> - **Action:** weight is transferred to front foot and the racket is thrown up and through the shuttle.
> - **Recovery:** the player follows through in the direction of the intended target.

VIDEO LINK

Head to www. brightredbooks.net/N5PE and watch the video clip of an overhead clear in badminton.

ONLINE TEST

How well have you learned about the characteristics of a skilled performance? Go online and test yourself at www.brightredbooks.net/N5PE

THINGS TO DO AND THINK ABOUT

Think about activities you have taken part in during your course. For each activity, choose one skill and break it down into preparation, action and recovery (PAR). Fill in the PAR sheet in Appendix 2 on p94 for each skill. Try to include four or five subroutines in each box.

You could also watch a video of someone else performing the skill and fill in a PAR sheet for them: the benefit is that you can watch the performance from different angles, and rewind and pause the video.

CLASSIFICATION OF SKILLS

When you are developing your skills, you need to be able to classify them according to different criteria. This will enable you to create practice routines that are best suited to improving your specific skill. Skills are usually:

- open or closed
- simple or complex
- continuous, discrete or serial

OPEN AND CLOSED SKILLS

Skills can be ranked on a **continuum** ranging from open to closed.

Closed ◄─────────────────────────────────► Open

1   2

Open skills

Open skills are unpredictable in nature. When performing open skills the environment is constantly changing and so movements have to be continually adapted. Pressure from outside factors – for example, opposition – usually means that the skills are externally paced.

Closed skills

Closed skills take place in a stable, predictable environment where the performer knows exactly what to do and when. Skills are not affected by the environment, and movements follow set patterns and have a clear beginning and end.

VIDEO LINK

Check out the 'Barcelona Possession 63 minute' clip – www.brightredbooks.net/N5PE

EXAMPLE 1   OPEN SKILL: PASSING IN FOOTBALL

Watch the video clip 'Barcelona Possession 63 minute'. In this clip, where Barcelona keeps possession of the football, the skill – in this case passing – is open. This is because the environment is continually changing and there is pressure from the opposition. Therefore, to deal with these constantly changing conditions, Barcelona use a variety of different passes – long, short, lofted and along the ground – to retain possession of the ball.

EXAMPLE 2   CLOSED SKILL: BASEKETBALL FREE THROW

Basketball free throws are closed skills, due to a number of characteristics. Free throws are always taken from the same point in any regulation court, therefore, the player knows what to expect when shooting and is able to rehearse a set routine for shooting a free throw. A free throw, unless played on an outdoor court, is unaffected by the weather.

However, not all skills are completely open or completely closed. A tee shot in golf, for example, is predominantly a closed skill because there is no direct pressure from opposition and the skill has a set movement pattern. It is external factors such as weather and layout of the course that make this skill more open. Golfers are required to play a variety of shots from the tee based on the type and layout of the hole. Also, as golf is an outdoor sport, it is affected by the weather, which makes the environment slightly more unpredictable.

SIMPLE OR COMPLEX SKILLS

Skills also vary from simple to complex. **Simple skills** contain a few, basic movements, which require few decisions to be made when they are executed.

Complex skills, on the other hand, usually require decisions to be made and a movement pattern to be selected from a range of possible choices. The movement pattern usually contains a number of difficult or complex movements to be carried out for the skill to be successful.

Whether a skill is simple or complex depends on the:

- number of decisions to be made
- **speed** at which the decisions must be made
- difficulty of the movement(s)
- accuracy required for the movement to be successful.

EXAMPLE SIMPLE SKILL
- Inside foot pass
- Chest pass
- Forward roll

EXAMPLE COMPLEX SKILL
- Back flip
- Tumble turn
- Triple jump

CONTINUOUS, DISCRETE OR SERIAL SKILLS

Continuous skills

Continuous skills have no obvious beginning or end and are repetitive. Examples include cycling, swimming and running.

Cycling – a continuous skill

Discrete skills

This skill has an obvious beginning and end. For example, with a hockey penalty flick, the skill begins when the flick has been taken and ends when the ball leaves contact with the stick. Other examples are a badminton serve and goal shooting in netball.

Hockey penalty flick – a discrete skill

Serial skills

Serial skills link **discrete skills** together. A triple jumper must link their approach run-up, take-off and step-and-jump to create as much **power** as possible to achieve maximum distance. Other examples are bowling in cricket and throwing the javelin.

Triple jump – a serial skill

 THINGS TO DO AND THINK ABOUT

1. Think of skills you perform in the activities on your course.

   Can you place these skills on the open to closed continuum? Give reasons for each of your answers.

   One way you could do this is to make a table with three columns: one column for open skills, one column for closed skills and one column for skills that share characteristics of both.

2. Create a spider diagram for both simple and complex skills. Add skills you can think of, or those you have performed on your course, to this diagram.

 DON'T FORGET

Athletes often demonstrate a variety of skill types in any one performance.

ONLINE TEST

How well have you learned about the classification of skills? Go online and test yourself at www.brightredbooks.net/N5PE

ASPECTS OF FITNESS IMPACTING ON PERFORMANCE 1

DEMANDS OF PERFORMANCE

There are three **types of fitness** that can influence or have an impact on how we perform within an activity. These three types of fitness are **physical, skill-related** and **mental.** Within these three types there are various **aspects of fitness.** The table below shows the three types of fitness and the aspects within them.

	TYPE OF FITNESS		
	PHYSICAL	SKILL-RELATED	MENTAL
Aspects of fitness	• Stamina • Speed • Local muscular endurance • Strength • Power • Flexibility	• Balance • Coordination • Agility • Reaction time • Timing	• Managing anxiety and stress • Rehearsal • Level of arousal • Concentration • Determination

Different sporting activities require different types and aspects of fitness. For example, a 1500m runner will require the following;

- Physical fitness: stamina and speed
- Skill-related fitness: **coordination** and **balance**
- Mental fitness: managing emotions and mental rehearsal

However, this may vary from one athlete to the next.

Let's look first at the **physical aspects of fitness** and what they mean.

PHYSICAL ASPECTS OF FITNESS IN PERFORMANCE

Stamina

- Stamina is the ability as an athlete to transport sufficient oxygen to the working muscles during sustained exercise such as a 1500m race.
- Stamina allows the body to work for an extended period of time without fatigue setting in.
- Stamina enables you to maintain a steady pace for the duration of the race.
- Stamina means that your split times will be consistent.
- Stamina affects how early you will tire in the race and enables you to run faster for longer.
- Stamina affects whether you will be able to have a strong finish at the end of the race.
- Stamina affects your finishing position in the 1500m.
- Stamina affects your finishing time in the 1500m.

 **ACTIVITY:**

Think of other sporting activities where stamina might be important to your performance.

Speed

- Speed is the ability to cover a distance or perform a movement quickly.
- Speed affects your ability to have a quick start so that you can get in a good position early in the race.
- Speed affects your ability to overtake other athletes and to deny other athletes the chance to overtake you.
- Speed affects your ability to have a good fast finish.

contd

Strength

Strength is the maximum amount of force a muscle, or a group of muscles, can exert in a single effort. The amount of force depends on the size of the muscle. The larger the muscle, the stronger the force is.

Gymnast performing on the pommel horse

- **Dynamic strength** – This is the muscular strength a sports person needs to support their own body over a prolonged period of time, or to be able to apply force against some type of object. This type of strength is closely linked to **endurance** because the muscles need to work continuously.
- **Static strength** – This is the greatest amount of force which can be applied to an immovable object. This is important in any activity where you have to brace yourself against another performer, object or weight.

Rugby scrum

Sprinter

- **Explosive strength** – This is muscular strength used in one short, sharp movement. A sprinter leaving the starting blocks uses a great deal of explosive strength to push forwards and upwards as quickly as possible.

Power

Power is the combination of strength and speed. Power is increased using more strength and speed. Explosive power is where you use maximum, or almost maximum, strength and speed.

Flexibility

Flexibility is the range of movement through a joint. There are two types of flexibility: static and dynamic.

- **Static flexibility** – An example of static flexibility would be a gymnast attempting to perform the splits: they would transition into the movement and then hold their body in a fixed position.
- **Dynamic flexibility** – Dynamic flexibility describes the range and pace of a person's movements.

 DON'T FORGET

Power is needed in many sports. The main source of power comes from the working muscles in the arms and the legs.

ONLINE

Check out two great examples of power – a high jumper and a long jumper – at www.brightredbooks.net/N5PE

 THINGS TO DO AND THINK ABOUT

1. Think about a physical activity that you do and try to work out when you are using static, explosive or dynamic strength. Which type of strength do you use most?

2. Can you think of more examples where power is important?

 ONLINE TEST

Take the 'Aspects of fitness impacting on performance' test online at www.brightredbooks.net/N5PE

ASPECTS OF FITNESS IMPACTING ON PERFORMANCE 2

 **ACTIVITY** THE ROLE OF PHYSICAL ASPECTS OF FITNESS ON PERFORMANCE

Choose one physical aspect of fitness which is important within an activity in your course. Identify and explain the role this plays within your performance. Look at the table below for some examples.

EXAMPLE

Physical Aspect Of Fitness	Role And Explanation
Cardio-respiratory endurance or stamina	**Runner** Effective cardio-respiratory endurance is the ability to transport sufficient oxygen to the working muscles during sustained exercise.
Local muscular endurance	**Rower** The rower uses his arm and leg muscles repeatedly, over a long period of time.
Speed	**Sprinter** The sprinter drives hard with her arms and legs to gain speed.
Strength	**Rugby** The prop in rugby needs strength to gain an advantage over their opponent in the scrum.
Power	**Athletics** The high jumper needs power in the take-off phase in his jump.
Flexibility	**Golfer** The golfer requires good shoulder and hip flexibility to turn efficiently in the back swing and follow through. Flexibility is the range of movement which is possible through a joint.

SKILL-RELATED ASPECTS OF FITNESS IN PERFORMANCE

Now that you've learned about the physical aspects of fitness that have an impact on performance, let's have a look at the **skill-related aspects**.

Balance

● Balance is the ability to retain the centre of gravity over your base of support.

● Balance requires you to control different muscle groups

● Balance, for example, is particularly vital at the start of a race when there are many athletes jostling for position. If you are bumped and don't retain your balance, you might not get off to a good start. If you are bumped during the race it is also crucial to retain balance: if you don't, you might not be able to stay in the race.

contd

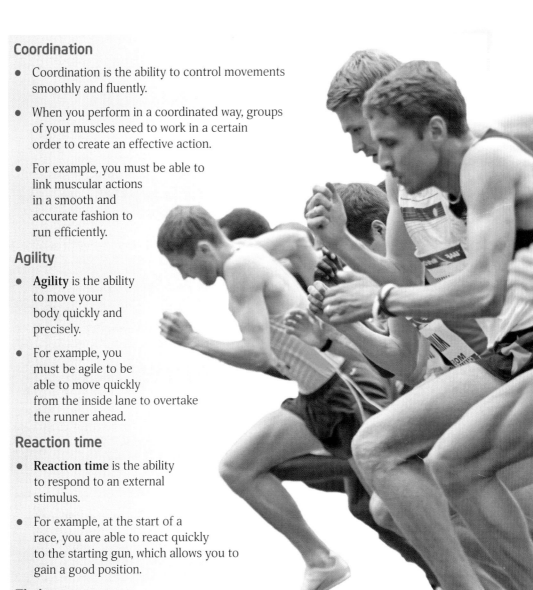

Coordination

- Coordination is the ability to control movements smoothly and fluently.

- When you perform in a coordinated way, groups of your muscles need to work in a certain order to create an effective action.

- For example, you must be able to link muscular actions in a smooth and accurate fashion to run efficiently.

Agility

- **Agility** is the ability to move your body quickly and precisely.

- For example, you must be agile to be able to move quickly from the inside lane to overtake the runner ahead.

Reaction time

- **Reaction time** is the ability to respond to an external stimulus.

- For example, at the start of a race, you are able to react quickly to the starting gun, which allows you to gain a good position.

Timing

- **Timing** is the ability to perform skills or movements at the right time with the correct purpose.

- For example, if you are swimming and perform a tumble turn, you have to time this perfectly. If you turn too early you will end up being too far away from the wall to fully push off the wall and maintain your speed. If you turn too late you will probably lose speed and possibly injure yourself.

 THINGS TO DO AND THINK ABOUT

Think of other sporting activities where skill-related aspects of fitness are important to performance.

 VIDEO LINK

Head to www.brightredbooks.net/N5PE and watch the video on the reaction times of a professional baseball player.

DON'T FORGET

Professional athletes must master a huge range of skills if they wish to succeed.

 ONLINE TEST

Take the 'Aspects of fitness impacting on performance' test online at www.brightredbooks.net/N5PE

ASPECTS OF FITNESS IMPACTING ON PERFORMANCE 3

MENTAL ASPECTS OF FITNESS IN PERFORMANCE

Now that you've learned about the physical and skill-related aspects of fitness that have an impact on performance, let's have a look at the **mental aspects**.

Level of arousal

Arousal levels in sport are important.

Too little arousal causes the level of involvement to be low. If the level of arousal is too high, it could result in loss of control.

Studies have shown that there is an optimum level of arousal. This has produced the 'Inverted U' theory and clearly links levels of performance with levels of arousal.

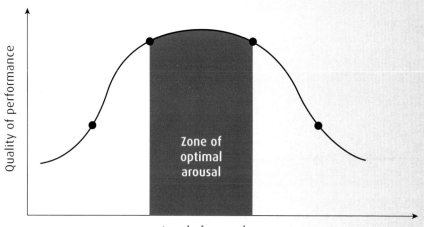

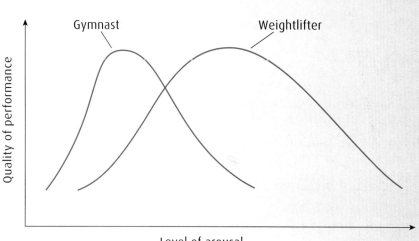

DON'T FORGET

Different sports and sportspeople require different arousal levels. A shot putter will have to raise their arousal level before stepping into the circle. A snooker player will need to keep their arousal level low before striking the cue ball.

contd

The relationship between arousal and performance can be complicated. While one person might need to be 'psyched up' for the challenge of competition, another might 'choke' and perform far below expectations.

As a sports athlete, you need to learn to control arousal. You should be able to increase arousal when feeling lethargic (tired) and decrease it when the pressure causes nervousness and anxiety.

It is the better athletes who are able to control arousal when they perform in anxiety-provoking games.

Managing anxiety and stress

Anxiety is an emotional state, similar to **fear**. It is associated with physiological and psychological arousal and with feelings of nervousness and apprehension.

Concentration

Concentration is the ability to completely focus your attention on something for a period of time. When athletes concentrate well they can take in all the information they need to make good decisions such as responding to their opponent or adapting to their environment.

Ideally, you'll reach a state where your performance just flows.

Determination

Determination is the desire and drive to improve in your particular sport.

Determination helps you to be the best that you can be.

ONLINE

Complete the anxiety test, more commonly known as the SCAT test online at www.brightredbooks.net/N5PE

THINGS TO DO AND THINK ABOUT

Think of some times when you have felt determined to succeed within your sport. What impact did this have on your performance? Was it positive or negative?

 ONLINE TEST

Take the 'Aspects of fitness impacting on performance' test online at www.brightredbooks.net/N5PE

FEEDBACK

Feedback is the information you receive about your performance. Feedback occurs after you have executed a skill. It can be generated by your senses (feeling, sight, sound) or it can come from a coach or someone watching your performance. The type of feedback you get depends on the type of task you are completing, the type of skills being performed and the nature of the activity.

TYPES OF FEEDBACK

There are two types of feedback: intrinsic (internal) and **extrinsic** (external).

Intrinsic feedback

The performer gets intrinsic or internal feedback from the feelings in their muscles and joints, and from their sense of balance as a direct result of carrying out a skill. This is often referred to as **kinaesthetic awareness**.

Extrinsic feedback

Extrinsic or external feedback comes in the following forms:

- Written – for example, an observation schedule, personal performance sheet or personal reflection sheet.
- Verbal – for example, from a coach, teacher or team mate (unbiased).
- Visual – for example, from video analysis or a model performer.

Extrinsic feedback gives added information to the intrinsic feedback provided by your senses. There are two main categories:

1 **Knowledge of performance (KP).** This is information about the technique and performance. It can be provided verbally from an observer or visually, via video. It allows you to gain feedback from someone who is seeing your performance from a different perspective.

2 **Knowledge of results (KR).** This is information that relates to the outcome of your performance – for example, your 100-metre sprint time, whether or not you scored a free throw in basketball or where a cross ends up in football.

Beginners often rely on a lot of extrinsic feedback when they are developing and improving their skill level. However, as performers become more experienced, they learn to pick out key pieces of intrinsic feedback.

ONLINE TEST

Take the 'Feedback' test online at www. brightredbooks.net/N5PE

CHARACTERISTICS OF EXTRINSIC FEEDBACK

Extrinsic feedback should:

- reinforce positive aspects of a performance and suggest areas in which a performance might be improved
- be constructive and have specific points on how the performance can be improved
- be relevant to the ability and stage of the performer (for example, someone just beginning football should be given simple, easy-to-follow feedback, whereas a professional will receive more complex, technical feedback)
- ideally focus on two or three main points at a time, so as not to overload the performer with information.

Extrinsic feedback is information received from others observing your performance.

DON'T FORGET

Intrinsic feedback is received from your kinaesthetic senses (where your body feels different parts of the action).

USING INTRINSIC AND EXTRINSIC FEEDBACK

EXAMPLE   FOOTBALL

In football, when completing a cross into the box, you receive internal feedback about the action through kinaesthetic senses. Your senses will tell you how balanced you were when you delivered the cross, how good your timing was and how well you connected with the ball. As you practise and improve at crossing, you will develop a feeling and awareness of when you have produced an effective cross.

You will also receive extrinsic feedback about the cross. The main extrinsic feedback will be the outcome of the cross itself – that is, did the cross go to the intended target? This is called **knowledge of results**. Your teacher o coach can also provide information about the positive aspects of the cross and how you could improve your technique in future. This is called **knowledge of performance.**

For additional extrinsic feedback, you could record your performance and analyse it after your training session. Using this type of feedback allows you to rewind, slow down or pause the performance so you can break the skill down and analyse the different parts.

VIDEO LINK

Head to www. brightredbooks.net/N5PE to watch the video clip of Rory McIlroy hitting a tee shot. When you watch the video you can see that almost immediately after McIlroy strikes the golf ball, he can tell that it is a bad shot. What type(s) of feedback has Rory McIlroy received to tell him that he has played a bad tee shot?

EXTRINSIC FEEDBACK: KNOWLEDGE OF PERFORMANCE TABLE

During practice sessions, the learning environment allows coaches or teachers to stop play and offer performers instant feedback on a skill. However, during competitive matches the environment is open and fast-paced. Therefore, performers are rarely able to receive and process feedback on their performance. In cases such as these, Knowledge of Performance (KP) can be used by a performer to analyse their performance after the event has finished.

These KP tables are examples of this. They look in detail at key skills used during the game, rather than focusing solely on the end result. These tables could be completed for a whole team or for individuals as shown below.

	JOHN	DAVID	MIKE	TERRY
Passes complete	5	8	11	4
Turn overs	0	3	1	7
Successful 2pt shots	3	11	7	9
Successful 3pt shots	1	0	2	2
Rebounds	2	0	1	1
Blocks	1	1	0	0

TEAM A	SKILL	TEAM B
65	Passes complete	72
15	Turn overs	9
27	Successful 2pt shots	29
3	Successful 3pt shots	5
5	Rebounds	7
1	Blocks	3

DON'T FORGET

Feedback and motivation are linked. Receiving positive feedback on your performance is likely to motivate you to continue in that activity.

THINGS TO DO AND THINK ABOUT

1   Think about the skills you have learnt so far on your course. Discuss how you could tell when you first executed a skill correctly/successfully.

2   After reading 'Types of feedback' place your answers for question 1 under either intrinsic feedback or extrinsic feedback.

3   A good example of experiencing intrinsic feedback is during a basketball free throw. Try shooting 10 free throws with a partner. Each time you shoot close your eyes just after you have released the ball and try to guess whether the ball will go into the hoop using your kinaesthetic senses. (Your partner can tell you if you were correct.) See how many shots you can guess correctly.

THE CYCLE OF ANALYSIS

The Cycle of Analysis is one of the most popular approaches used to investigate, analyse and develop your performance. It enables you to follow straightforward steps that will help you to structure a performance improvement programme and avoid **learning plateaus**.

THE FOUR STAGES OF THE CYCLE OF ANALYSIS

The four stages of the Cycle of Analysis are:

1. Investigate

To investigate, you should gather information about your performance using different methods (see pp26–41 for more on these methods).

2. Analyse

This stage involves using the information you have gathered to identify strengths and areas that need development in your performance.

3. Develop

The next stage is to create a development programme that helps improve your weaknesses.

4. Evaluate

To evaluate, you should reflect on how effective your development programme was in helping you to identify and improve areas of weakness and think about any future development needs.

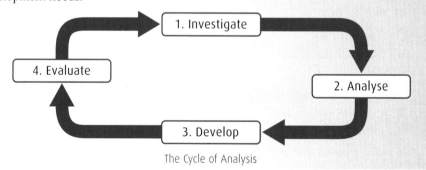

The Cycle of Analysis

TYPES OF DATA

During the investigation process, you will be required to gather data on your performance. Data comes in two forms:

- Objective data
- Subjective data

Objective data

Objective data is information or results that come from controlled tests – for example, the Multistage Fitness Test, number of passes complete. Objective data is usually precise and can be compared to that of peers or to National Average results.

Subjective data

Subjective data is based more on an element of opinion or personal feeling – for example, feeling tired during a match or competition. Subjective data is vaguer than objective data, and can be difficult to compare accurately.

We'll look at how to gather and use both objective and subjective data in the next few pages.

LEARNING PLATEAUS

By using the Cycle of Analysis, learning plateaus can be avoided. A learning plateau is when you feel that you are no longer making any improvement in your performance. The graph to the right illustrates a learning plateau. When they are taking part in activities, learners often experience a quick improvement in basic performance. However, their learning often plateaus over time due to a range of factors. The following example shows a question about learning plateaus that could come up in the course assessment.

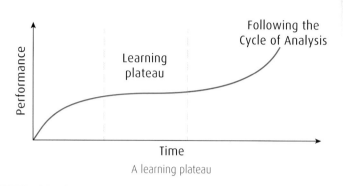

A learning plateau

EXAMPLE   ASSESSMENT QUESTION

1. Can you think of reasons why you may encounter a learning plateau?
It is important to consider a number of factors to prevent or reduce the chances of a learning plateau occurring. There are several physical, skill-related and mental factors that can contribute to this happening. It is also important to consider the stage of learning and the method of practice that you are planning on using within your training programme. Here is a possible answer to this question:

When creating my training programme to improve my forehand topspin I must ensure that the practices I use are appropriate to the stage of learning that I am at. See the three stages of learning below.

At the cognitive stage of learning I used simple practices that allowed me to work on the individual subroutines of the forehand topspin. Subroutines are the components that make up a skill or a series of movements that link together to perform a skill. I chose to use both the shadow and basic repetition practices because there is very little pressure and little movement required and I can use different forms of external feedback to help me improve.

Shadow practice is a method of practice where you perform the sequence of movements that make up a forehand topspin, without the added pressure of returning the ball. In doing so it allows me to groove muscle memory, which helps my overall technique to improve. I can also refer to a model performer throughout this practice as this will provide me with a mental image of performing the shot correctly. Using a model performer also acts as a motivation as I would be aiming to play the shot as well as them after my training programme is complete. While this method can become quite tedious, it is important that the performer goes through this process when trying to improve a new skill. By ensuring that I can perform all of the subroutines correctly, I am then able to progress onto more challenging but achievable practices. This is another reason that a learning plateau may occur. The methods of practices used may be too difficult or too easy at each of the stages of learning, and this could demotivate me and result in my performance not improving and a learning plateau occurring.

The seven principles of effective practice should also be considered to prevent a learning plateau:

- *Intensity*
- *Work-to-rest ratio*
- *Achievable progressive stages*
- *Strengths and weaknesses*
- *Awareness of skilled performer*
- *Clear objectives*
- *Effect of boredom and fatigue*

Another way of structuring your answer to this question would be to place the reasons into three categories:

- physical
- skill-related
- mental

Once you have categorised your reasons, expand your answer by putting it in paragraph form like the example above.

THINGS TO DO AND THINK ABOUT

The Cycle of Analysis is an ongoing process. To maintain progress, the cycle should be repeated so that you are continually monitoring and working to improve areas of weakness.

GATHERING INFORMATION ABOUT PHYSICAL FACTORS 1

There are several ways that you can gather information on your performance and the factors that impact on your performance. By using a variety of methods, you will be able to assess your current level of fitness and the demands of your performance.

GENERAL OVERVIEW OF FACTORS

This approach allows you to gain an initial understanding of all the factors that impact on your performance by looking at each factor in turn. By completing a General Overview of Factors sheet like the one below, you can gain a better understanding of where your strengths and areas for improvement lie. You can then investigate specific factors in more detail using some of the tests mentioned in this chapter.

PHYSICAL FACTORS	SOCIAL FACTORS	MENTAL FACTORS	EMOTIONAL FACTORS
Do you get tired towards the end of your performance?	Do you get along with everyone who is involved in your activity: for example, team mates, coach, referee?	Do you lose concentration at any stage during performance?	Do you ever feel anxious or nervous when performing?
Can you successfully carry out all the skills required to perform effectively?	Do you always follow the rules of the activity during performance?	Do you find it easy to make the correct decisions during performance?	Do you lose your temper during performance if you or someone in your team makes a mistake?
Do you understand the tactics that will allow you to beat an opponent in your activity?	Is your performance affected because there are limited facilities for you to train?	When performing, do you find it easy to remain mentally tough at all times?	Do you always approach an activity with a positive attitude?

STANDARDISED TESTING

Standardised tests are a very effective method of gathering information on performance. These tests all have set procedures and rules that ensure each test is carried out in the same way every time. This also ensures that the data gathered is reliable and that it is easy to compare your data with that of your peers or of national averages.

STANDARDISED PHYSICAL TESTS 1

EXAMPLE   MULTISTAGE FITNESS TEST

VIDEO LINK

Learn more about the Multistage Fitness Test by checking out the clip in the BrightRED Digital Zone.

The Multistage Fitness Test or Beep Test is a very common test that is used to measure your Cardio-Respiratory Endurance (CRE). Participants are required to run between lines or cones 20 m apart according to recorded 'beeps'. Initially, the time between beeps allows the participant to start at a slow pace. As they move up each level, the time between beeps decreases and the demands on participants increase. If a participant fails to reach the line on two occasions, they stop and record the level.

Use the table below to compare your own Multistage Fitness result to the national average for your age.

Male

Age	Excellent	Above average	Average	Below average	Poor
14–16	L12 S7	L11 S2	L8 S9	L7 S1	< L6 S6

Female

Age	Excellent	Above average	Average	Below average	Poor
14–16	L10 S9	L9 S1	L6 S7	L5 S1	< L4 S7

ONLINE TEST

How much do you know about this topic? Head to www.brightredbooks.net/ N5PE and take the 'Gathering information about physical factors' test.

DON'T FORGET

Participants in the Multistage Fitness Test can only fail to reach the line before the 'beep' sound on two occasions.

THINGS TO DO AND THINK ABOUT

Think about a sport you currently participate in and complete a General Overview of Factors sheet like the one on p26 about your performance in this sport. Can you gain a better understanding of where your strengths and areas for improvement lie after completing this sheet?

GATHERING INFORMATION ABOUT PHYSICAL FACTORS 2

STANDARDISED PHYSICAL TESTS 2

EXAMPLE STANDING BROAD JUMP

The Standing Broad Jump is a common test used for testing power in your legs. During the test, the participant performs a two-footed jump for distance. Each participant performs three jumps and takes their best result. The result is measured from the heel of the rear landing foot to the line the participant jumped from.

Use the table below to compare your Standing Broad Jump result to the national average for your age.

Male

Age	Excellent	Above average	Average	Below average	Poor
14	>2.11 m	2.11–1.96 m	1.95–1.85 m	1.84–1.68 m	<1.68 m
15	>2.26 m	1.26–2.11 m	2.10–1.98 m	1.97–1.85 m	<1.85 m
16	>2.36 m	2.36–2.21 m	2.20–2.11 m	2.10–1.98 m	<1.98 m

Female

Age	Excellent	Above average	Average	Below average	Poor
14	>1.91 m	1.91–1.73 m	1.72–1.60 m	1.59–1.47 m	<1.47 m
15	>1.85 m	1.84–1.73 m	1.72–1.60 m	1.59–1.50 m	<1.50 m
16	>1.83 m	1.83–1.68 m	1.67–1.58 m	1.57–1.45 m	<1.45 m

EXAMPLE SIT AND REACH

The Sit and Reach Test is used to measure the flexibility across your hip joint. The muscles involved are the hamstrings and lower back. To carry out the Sit and Reach Test you require either a Sit and Reach Box or a box and ruler. Participants are required to sit with their feet against the box and their legs straight and flat against the floor. Participants reach as far forward as they can, while keeping their legs flat on the floor. The test can be repeated and the best result recorded.

Use the table below to compare your Sit and Reach result to the national average for your age.

Gender	Excellent	Above average	Average	Below average	Poor
Male	>14 inches	14.0–11.0 inches	10.9–7.0 inches	6.9–4.0 inches	<4 inches
Female	>15 inches	15.0–12.0 inches	11.9–7.0 inches	6.9–4.0 inches	<4 inches

contd

EXAMPLE GRIP DYNAMOMETER

The grip strength dynamometer measures the amount of force you can exert in one single effort using hand and forearm strength. The participant gets three attempts and records their highest result (in kg).

Use the table below to compare your grip dynamometer result to the national average for your age.

Gender	Excellent	Good	Average	Fair	Poor
Male	>56 kg	51–56 kg	45–50 kg	39–44 kg	<39 kg
Female	>36 kg	31–36 kg	25–30 kg	19–24 kg	<19 kg

DON'T FORGET

The highest result of three attempts will be recorded in the grip dynamometer test.

STANDARDISED SKILL TESTS 1

EXAMPLE STORK TEST

The Stork Test is used to measure balance. Participants stand on their right leg and place the sole of their left foot on their knee cap. They then raise themselves up onto their tip toe and the clock starts. The clock stops if the participant moves their foot off their knee cap, or comes down from their tip toes. This test is then repeated for the other leg.

Use the table below to compare your Stork Test result for each leg to the national average for your age.

Rating	Males	Females
Excellent	>50 secs	>30 secs
Above average	41–50 secs	23–30 secs
Average	31–40 secs	16–22 secs
Below average	20–30 secs	10–15 secs
Poor	<20 secs	<10 secs

ONLINE TEST

How much do you know about this topic? Head to www.brightredbooks.net/N5PE and take the 'Gathering information about physical factors' test.

THINGS TO DO AND THINK ABOUT

Have a go at one of the standardised physical tests in this section. (Look back to p27 for the Multistage Fitness Test.) Then ask yourself:

- How well did I do?
- Was I higher or lower than the average result for my age and gender?

With this in mind, devise a few practices you can do to improve this skill.

GATHERING INFORMATION ABOUT PHYSICAL FACTORS 3

STANDARDISED SKILL TESTS 2

EXAMPLE ILLINOIS AGILITY

The Illinois Agility Test is used to measure your agility. The Illinois Agility can be conducted in a gym hall, playground or on a sports field. To the right is a diagram of how the Illinois Agility Test should be set up. Participants are required to start the test lying down on their front with their arms spread. The timer shouts 'go' and the participant runs the course as quickly as possible. The timer is stopped as soon as the participant crosses the finish line.

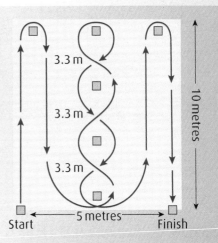

Use the table below to compare your Illinois Agility Test result to the national average for your age.

Gender	Excellent	Above average	Average	Below average	Poor
Male	<15.2 secs	15.2–16.1 secs	16.2–18.1 secs	18.2–19.3 secs	>19.3 secs
Female	<17.0 secs	17.0–17.9 secs	18.0–21.7 secs	21.8–23.0 secs	>23.0 secs

EXAMPLE RULE DROP

The Rule Drop measures your reaction time. The diagram to the right shows the procedure for the Rule Drop. A partner holds a 30 cm ruler with their thumb and forefinger and the participant places an open thumb and forefinger at the bottom of the ruler. When the partner drops the ruler the participant must catch the ruler as soon as they can between their thumb and forefinger, taking the result from where they catch the ruler.

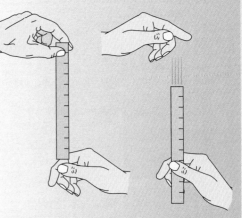

Use the table below to compare your Rule Drop result to the national average for your age.

Excellent	Above average	Average	Below average	Poor
<7.5 cm	7.5–15.9 cm	15.9–20.4 cm	20.4–28 cm	>28 cm

contd

ONLINE

Learn more about the tests mentioned and investigate other tests at www. brightredbooks.net/N5PE

EXAMPLE ALTERNATE BALL TOSS

The Alternate Ball Toss is used to measure hand–eye coordination. The participant stands two metres away from a flat wall with the ball in their right hand. They are required to throw the ball against the wall and catch it again in their left hand. The test is conducted over 30 seconds and the participant tries to complete as many throw and catches in that time.
Use the table below to compare your Alternate Ball Toss result to the national average for your age.

DON'T FORGET

A good sports performer will be able to score well in a variety of different standardised tests.

Age	High score	Above average	Average	Below average	Low score
15–16 years	>35	30 – 35	25 – 29	20 – 24	<20

 **ACTIVITY**

Investigate other standardised tests that are important to your chosen activity and complete the table below. Add more if you can think of others!

TEST	TYPE OF FITNESS	ASPECT OF FITNESS	RULES/PROCEDURES	EQUIPMENT
Cooper Test	Physical	CRE		Stop-watch, cones 400m track
Sergeant Jump		Power		
Harvard Step Test				
Scat Test	Mental	Anxiety		
Press-up Test	Physical	Local Muscular Endurance (LME)		
30m Sprint Test		Speed		
Shoulder Elevation Test		Flexibility		

 ## THINGS TO DO AND THINK ABOUT

Have a go at one of the standardised skills tests in this section. (Look back to p29 for the Stork Test.) Then ask yourself:

- How well did I do?
- Was I higher or lower than the average result for my age and gender?

With this in mind, devise a few practices you can do to improve this skill.

 ## ONLINE TEST

How much do you know about this topic? Head to www.brightredbooks.net/ N5PE and take the 'Gathering information about physical factors' test.

GATHERING INFORMATION ABOUT PHYSICAL FACTORS 4

Gathering information on the various aspects of physical fitness is important as we begin the process of improving and developing our performance.

DON'T FORGET

Remember that you are analysing and writing about **your own** performance for the portfolio.

VIDEO ANALYSIS

Recording your performance allows you to participate in an activity or perform a skill without having to think about analysis during the action, but helps you to analyse your performance afterwards. It provides effective feedback.

The advantages of recording your performance are that it can be:

- paused, slowed down and rewound
- easily stored
- used to track progress.

The advantages of video analysis are that it enables you to:

- view a model performance and compare it to your own
- highlight component parts of skills performed at a high pace or, in other words, to break a skill down
- observe a performance from different angles
- view your performance as others see it.

Recording your performance is also very useful when you are filling out an observation schedule.

DON'T FORGET

Observation schedules can be used to track your progress, so the **same** observation schedule should be filled out when first identifying your strengths and weaknesses and then used again a number of weeks later to record the improvements in your performance.

OBSERVATION SCHEDULES

Observation schedules are used to record information about your performance. They can be a particularly useful way of identifying your strengths and weaknesses in a certain activity. Observation schedules are usually completed by someone who is watching your performance. However, you can also video your performance and conduct your own observation schedule.

When designing an observation schedule, it is important to think about the criteria on which your performance will be judged – that is, what are you looking for in your performance? You would usually identify a model performer and compare your performance to theirs. It is vital that the information you collect from your observation schedule is **reliable**, **valid** and **easy to interpret**.

There are two types of observation schedule you can carry out:

- General
- Focused

General observation/performance sheet

This looks at your whole performance – for example, all your shots in table tennis. Using a general observation schedule will allow you to identify your strengths and weaknesses for the whole range of shots. See the observation sheet on p33.

ONLINE TEST

How much do you know about this topic? Head to www.brightredbooks.net/N5PE and take the 'Gathering information about physical factors' test.

General observation sheet				
My performance				
Observer's name:			**Date:**	
	Always	Usually	Sometimes	Never
Well-balanced.				
Relaxed, alert and ready.				
Covers the full table.				
Footwork is fluent. Can get to the right place at the table to hit the ball with relative ease and with time to play a 'good' shot.				
Footwork is light and quick.				
Agile. Demonstrates a good reach and recovery. Able to change direction easily				
Positioning is good. Recover to 'base' between shots.				
Good anticipation and reactions are quick.				
Uses a variety of strokes and forces opponent out of position to gain a strategic advantage.				
Capitalises on unforced opponent errors.				
Placement of shots is accurate.				
Shots show good quality of touch. Can use full or part-power as required.				
Can sustain long rallies and maintain the quality of shots.				
Can maintain control when pressured.				

Focused observation schedule

This looks in more detail at a specific technique. For a focused observation schedule you could break a skill down into key (component) parts to identify which part requires improvement – for example, breaking down an overhead clear into preparation, action and recovery. From this you can pinpoint certain areas of weakness in your technique – for example, transfer of weight from back foot to front foot during the overhead clear. You could use the sheet below to monitor your technique in a racquet sport.

Forehand																													
		good	OK	poor	good	OK	poor	good	OK	poor	good	OK	poor	good	OK	poor	good	OK	poor	good	OK	poor	good	OK	poor	good	OK	poor

Backhand																													
		good	OK	poor	good	OK	poor	good	OK	poor	good	OK	poor	good	OK	poor	good	OK	poor	good	OK	poor	good	OK	poor	good	OK	poor

THINGS TO DO AND THINK ABOUT

There are a number of apps you can use to record, slow down and analyse your performance. Here are some good (free) examples listed below (although there are lots of others available).

- *Coach My Video*
- *Ubersense*
- *Slowpro*

33

GATHERING INFORMATION ABOUT PHYSICAL FACTORS 5

MATCH AND GRID ANALYSIS

Match or game analysis is a useful way of using statistical information to analyse your game. A match analysis can be conducted over the duration of a single game or over a number of games in the season.

Below are two examples of how a match analysis can be used to help you analyse your (or your team's) strengths and weaknesses.

EXAMPLE MATCH ANALYSIS FOR TWO FOOTBALLERS DURING A SINGLE MATCH

Player A	Performance criteria	Player B
Offensive midfielder	Position	Centre midfielder
125	Total passes	111
113 (89%)	Accurate passes	108 (96%)
12 (8%)	Inaccurate passes	3 (1%)
64 (50%)	Forward passes	77 (68%)
61 (47%)	Backward passes	34 (29%)
57 (44%)	Accurate forward passes	73 (64%)
56 (43%)	Accurate backward passes	35 (30%)
4	Penetrating runs	0
3	Attempted assists	0
12	Lost balls	3

EXAMPLE MATCH ANALYSIS FOR A CRICKET TEAM OVER A SEASON

Bowling Statistics – Greenside Cricket Club (season 2011)

	Wides	No balls	Overs	Maidens	Runs	Wickets	Average	Strike rate	Economy rate
A Richard	13	2	108.3	28	300	32	9.38	3.38	2.77
J Roberts	1	9	59.2	6	259	23	11.26	2.57	4.38
G Aird	18	4	111.0	20	391	28	13.96	3.96	3.52
S North	1	0	67.0	11	231	15	15.40	4.47	3.45
S Austin	17	2	159.1	32	483	29	16.66	5.49	3.04
A Mirza	1	0	7.0	1	25	2	12.50	3.50	3.57
B Barratt	1	10	20.0	3	72	5	14.40	4.00	3.60
R Cousins	14	2	29.1	1	146	8	18.25	3.64	5.02

KNOWLEDGE OF RESULTS

Knowledge of results is also very useful as a measurement of performance. The information gained from your knowledge of results can be used to identify strengths and weaknesses in:

- aspects of fitness
- skill execution
- structure or strategy during a game.

EXAMPLE   KNOWLEDGE OF RESULTS – FOOTBALL

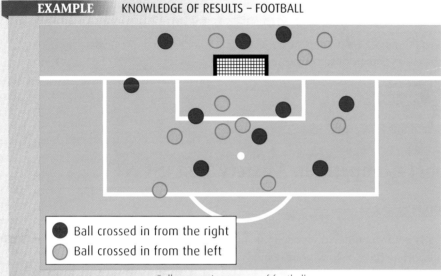

Ball crosses in a game of football

The diagram illustrates where the ball was crossed to during a game of football. Looking at the results, a range of conclusions can be drawn.

Aspects of fitness

Football requires excellent cardio-respiratory endurance (CRE). In the match illustrated above, 20 crosses were made. The diagram could indicate that as the wingers started to fatigue, their accuracy of cross dropped. A more detailed diagram could note the time at which the crosses were delivered to link fatigue during the match to accuracy of cross.

Skill execution

During the game only about 30 per cent (6 out of 20) of crosses were delivered into a goal-scoring area. A further 30 per cent of crosses went straight out of play. These results suggest a weakness in the players' crossing ability. Players, coaches and teachers can use this data to identify strengths and weaknesses and plan their training to develop these weaknesses.

Structure or strategy during a game

The information from the match could be used to review the team's attacking strategy. For example, the team may have chosen to use width as their game plan to pull the defence wide and cross the ball to the strikers in the box. Looking at the data after the game, coaches and players can evaluate their decisions – was using width the right strategy? Would it have been more effective to play the ball through the middle? Was the players' skill level high enough to play this strategy?

 DON'T FORGET

A match analysis can be conducted over the duration of a single game or over a number of games in the season. Each method has its own benefits and it is best to use both!

 ONLINE TEST

Test how well you know this topic by taking the 'Gathering information about physical factors' test online at www. brightredbooks.net/N5PE

 VIDEO LINK

Follow the 'Women's Hockey' link at www.brightredbooks. net/N5PE and complete the match analysis grid provided.

 THINGS TO DO AND THINK ABOUT

1 Can you think of the advantages of carrying out a match analysis over the duration of a single game?

2 Why would you want to conduct a match analysis over a number of games during the season?

GATHERING INFORMATION ABOUT MENTAL FACTORS

SPORT COMPETITION ANXIETY TEST (SCAT)

A Sports Competition Anxiety Test (SCAT) is a test designed to calculate how anxious a sportsperson gets prior to competing.

Complete this SCAT test:

Sport Competition Anxiety Test (SCAT)

Assessing your anxiety

Read the 15 statements below and decide if each one applies to you 'rarely', 'sometimes' or 'often'. Tick the appropriate box to show your response.

	Rarely	Sometimes	Often
1. Competing against others is socially enjoyable.	☐	☐	☐
2. Before I compete I feel uneasy.	☐	☐	☐
3. Before I compete I worry about not performing well.	☐	☐	☐
4. I am a good sportsman when I compete.	☐	☐	☐
5. When I compete I worry about making mistakes.	☐	☐	☐
6. Before I compete I am calm.	☐	☐	☐
7. Setting a goal is important when competing.	☐	☐	☐
8. Before I compete I get a queasy feeling in my stomach.	☐	☐	☐
9. Just before competing I notice my heart beats faster than usual.	☐	☐	☐
10. I like to compete in games that demand a lot of physical energy.	☐	☐	☐
11. Before I compete I feel relaxed.	☐	☐	☐
12. Before I compete I am nervous.	☐	☐	☐
13. Team sports are more exciting than individual sports.	☐	☐	☐
14. I get nervous wanting to start the game.	☐	☐	☐
15. Before I compete I usually get uptight.	☐	☐	☐

Athlete's name _____

SCAT Score ☐

contd

Sport Competition Anxiety Test (SCAT)

Analysis

The score for the response to each question is detailed below. Enter the score for each question in the Athlete's Score column and then total the column up to provide a SCAT score.

Note that questions 1, 4, 7, 10 and 13 score zero regardless of the response.

Question No	Rarely	Sometimes	Often	Athlete's Score
1	0	0	0	
2	1	2	3	
3	1	2	3	
4	0	0	0	
5	1	2	3	
6	3	2	1	
7	0	0	0	
8	1	2	3	
9	1	2	3	
10	0	0	0	
11	3	2	1	
12	1	2	3	
13	0	0	0	
14	1	2	3	
15	1	2	3	

Total [   ]

SCAT Score **Analysis**

Less than 17   You have a low level of anxiety.
17 to 24   You have an average level of anxiety.
More than 24   You have a high level of anxiety.

CONCENTRATION

Concentration is another aspect of the mental factor of fitness that must be considered if you want to improve your performance. If you are unable to remain focused while you are in a competitive situation, you might not be able to perform to the best of your ability.

Can you think of times during a game, match or performance where you have not been able to focus fully? Do you think this affected your performance?

THINGS TO DO AND THINK ABOUT

Think about your score from the SCAT test. Now consider the following questions:

- Do you have a high, average or low level of anxiety?
- How do you feel this affects your performance?
- Is there anything you can do to improve your ability to cope with your anxiety levels to benefit your performance?

ONLINE

Follow the 'Concentration and Skills' link at www.brightredbooks.net/N5PE and complete the test.

ONLINE TEST

Test how well you know this topic by taking the 'Gathering information about mental factors' test online at www.brightredbooks.net/N5PE

DON'T FORGET

The ability to keep concentrating while feeling stressed is a key skill of a good performer.

GATHERING INFORMATION ABOUT EMOTIONAL FACTORS 1

PROFILE OF MOOD STATUS (POMS)

ONLINE

To take the POMS test visit the link at www. brightredbooks.net/N5PE

The Profile of Mood Status, commonly referred to as 'POMS', is a psychological test that asks you how you have been feeling in the week leading up to a performance. You are given a list of statements and are asked to choose the one that reflects most closely how you feel. For example:

Feeling	How I have felt
tense	not at all
	a little
	moderately
	quite a lot
	extremely

You can use your test results to gauge your levels of tension, depression, **anger**, vigour, fatigue and confusion.

Use the table below to compare your POMS result to the national average for athletes at a similar level.

DON'T FORGET

International competitors are more used to competing regularly and so display, on average, less negative moods than club-level competitors. Recreational competitors have less at stake than club or international level competitors and therefore display, on average, the least anger and depression ahead of a performance.

GROUP	TENSION	DEPRESSION	ANGER	VIGOUR	FATIGUE	CONFUSION
International	5.66	4.38	6.24	18.51	5.37	4.00
Club	9.62	8.67	9.91	15.64	8.16	7.38
Recreational	6.00	3.11	3.60	17.78	6.37	4.84

OBSERVATION SCHEDULE

POSITIVE BODY LANGUAGE			POSITIVE REACTION TO DECISIONS			POSITIVE COMMUNICATION		POSITIVE TEAM WORK		
Cheer	Smile	Celebrate	Acceptance			Verbal	Non-Verbal	Inclusive	Fulfilling your role	
✔ ✔ ✔		✔				✔ ✔				
✔ ✔						✔				

contd

NEGATIVE BODY LANGUAGE			NEGATIVE REACTION TO DECISION			NEGATIVE COMMUNICATION		NEGATIVE TEAM WORK		
Eyes look down	Shoulders down	Hunched over	Anger	Frustration	Question decision	Verbal	Non-verbal	Exclusion	Failing to fulfil your role	
✔✔✔✔ ✔✔✔	✔✔✔✔ ✔✔✔		✔✔✔✔ ✔✔	✔✔✔✔ ✔✔✔					✔✔✔✔ ✔✔	
	✔✔		✔✔✔✔ ✔✔	✔		✔✔		✔		
						✔		✔✔✔		
✔✔✔✔ ✔✔		✔✔✔✔						✔✔✔		
✔✔✔✔ ✔✔			✔✔✔ ✔✔							
	✔✔✔		✔✔✔							
			✔✔							
	✔✔✔	✔✔✔✔								

1st Quarter
2nd Quarter
3rd Quarter
4th Quarter

ONLINE TEST

Test how well you know this topic by taking the 'Gathering information about emotional factors' test online at www.brightredbooks.net/N5PE

THINGS TO DO AND THINK ABOUT

Carry out a Profile of Mood Status over the week leading up to your next performance. You can follow the link at www.brightredbooks.net/N5PE to complete the test online. Think about your results and consider the following questions:

- Are your results higher, lower or on a level with the national average?
- How do you feel these results affect your performance? Is there anything you can do to improve on your mood status in the lead up to a performance to improve your chances of success?

GATHERING INFORMATION ABOUT EMOTIONAL FACTORS 2

PERSONAL REFLECTION SHEET

Initial data

You should use your own internal thoughts and feelings about your performance to analyse your emotions around the performance and identify areas for improvement.

MY PERFORMANCE				
			Date:	
Before performance	**Always**	**Usually**	**Sometimes**	**Never**
I feel nervous before a game/ performance.				
I always feel relaxed and ready.				
I approach a match/performance with confidence.				
I feel excited before a match/performance.				
During performance				
I accept advice from coaches.				
I feel frustrated when I/my team make mistakes.				
I deal well with pressure during a game.				
I try my hardest even when I/my team are losing.				
I accept the referee's decisions.				
I encourage my team mates.				
After performance				
I shake hands with the opposition whether I win or lose.				
I get upset if I/my team lose.				

ANALYSING DATA

It is important to analyse information or data that you have gathered on your performance because it helps you to consider all the factors that have had both a positive and negative impact on that performance. This will, therefore, help you to highlight areas of strength and weakness and to consider what steps you need to take next. The personal reflection sheet above will help you to consider your own thoughts and opinions on your own performances. Analysing data such as standardised testing is simple, as it is a case of comparing your result to the national average. However, other data can require more detailed analysis and interpretation of the results.

Analysing data comes in many different forms such as:

- Video analysis
- Model performer
- Observation schedules.

contd

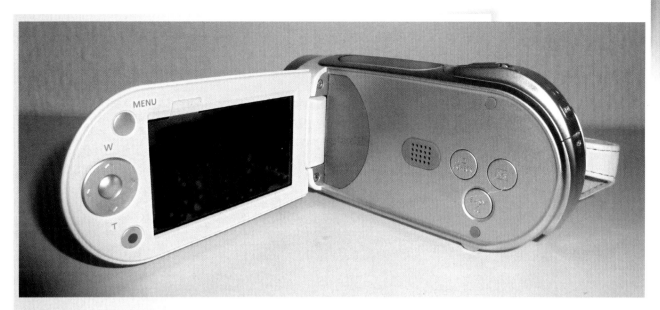

Video analysis

Video analysis is a very useful method of analysing data as it can provide you with instant feedback on your performance. Your coach might sit down with you and analyse your performance in greater detail, which will enable you to make relevant improvements/changes for the next time. Read more about video analysis on p32.

Model performer

You can also analyse data from a video to help you compare your own performance to a model performer. Watching a model performer allows you to identify key areas/skills which they perform well, and to compare these to the same areas/skills in your own performance. Some apps for tablets and computers are particularly useful as they allow you to split the screen and have the model performer on one side and you performing the same skill on the other.

However, the use of **visual** feedback (video of model performer) and **verbal** feedback (coach) might not suit everyone. It is important to establish which method(s) are best suited to you as a performer.

Observation schedules

Analysing data gathered from an observation schedule is a form of **written** feedback. This can be useful when you are trying to identify a weakness within a structure or strategy, or in a particular skill or technique within your activity. For example, an observation schedule could be used to identify that when you are trying to execute a dig in volleyball, your footwork is an area for improvement.

DON'T FORGET

Every person responds differently to different types of feedback. Not everything may work well for you. It is important to establish which method(s) are best suited to you as a performer.

ONLINE TEST

Test how well you know this topic by taking the 'Gathering information about emotional factors' test online at www.brightredbooks.net/N5PE

THINGS TO DO AND THINK ABOUT

Using the information you have gathered from the tests and observation schedules in this chapter, can you now identify your:

- strengths
- areas for improvement?

PHYSICAL FACTORS 1

There are many factors that can have a positive or negative impact on an individual's or teams' performance. In this chapter we will look at the physical, mental, emotional and social factors that affect our performances and possible ways of overcoming or minimising their impact.

INTRODUCTION

There are many physical factors that impact on performance. These include:

- Cardio-respiratory endurance (CRE)
- Speed
- Strength
- **Local muscular endurance** (LME)

The next few pages will explain each of the above factors and what effects they can have on performance.

CARDIO-RESPIRATORY ENDURANCE (CRE)

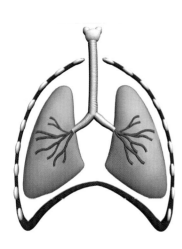

CRE is the ability of the heart and lungs to transport oxygenated blood to the working muscles around the body. The heart is a muscle which acts like a pump. When you begin to exercise, your heart needs to pump faster because the working muscles require more blood and oxygen to work efficiently. As your fitness improves, so does your heart's ability to work efficiently and to recover quickly too.

The lungs are the main organs of the respiratory system. The lungs are like two balloons that expand and constrict when you breathe. As you inhale oxygen through your nose and mouth, it travels down the trachea. Your trachea divides into two tubes called the bronchi, each one of which enters a lung. The bronchi then branch out into small air-filled sacs called alveoli. Here, the oxygen you breathed in passes into the blood stream, where it is sent to the working muscles and organs around the body. We breathe out carbon dioxide. This bi-product is produced once cells within the body breakdown nutrients. Carbon dioxide passes from the blood stream to the alveoli.

How can CRE impact positively on your performance?

When your heart and lungs are fit and strong, CRE will impact positively on your performance. It allows you to sustain high-intensity exercise for long periods of time before fatigue sets in. Your body is also able to recover much more quickly when your heart and lungs are fit.

> **EXAMPLE**   FOOTBALL
>
> When playing Centre Midfield (CM) in football, it is important that you have a high level of CRE. This will allow you to track back and help in defence, and also allow you to **support** the attackers. The CM player is considered the engine room of many teams, because they usually control the **tempo** of the game. The player that has this quality will be able to sustain a high tempo of play throughout the game in both an attacking and defensive sense.

How can CRE impact negatively on your performance?

If your heart and lungs are not working as efficiently as they could be, this will have a negative impact on your performance.

contd

> **EXAMPLE** BADMINTON
>
> In badminton, poor CRE might mean that you find it difficult to recover to the base position after every shot during long rallies. Your opponent can then capitalise on this by hitting the shuttle into the gaps created by your inability to recover quickly enough, and you will therefore lose more points.

 ACTIVITY

Think of activities that you have participated in throughout your course that require a high level of CRE.

- How might you improve your CRE?
- How would you know if your CRE had improved or not over a period of time?

SPEED

What is speed?

Speed is 'the ability to move the body and/or its parts quickly.' For the body to move at speed, both arms and legs must move in an energy-efficient way. This creates maximum output with a minimal amount of effort/energy.

> **EXAMPLE** 100 m SPRINTER
>
> A 100 m sprinter requires a high level of speed to perform well in their event. They also have to react quickly to the starting gun before they can move: this is more commonly known as reaction time.

How can speed impact positively on your performance?

High speed improves performance in a number of sports.

> **EXAMPLE** VOLLEYBALL
>
> In volleyball, it is important that each player possesses a high enough level of speed to enable them to move quickly into the correct position, in relation to the ball. Because they are not sure where the ball will be played next, it is vital that they are able to move quickly as and when they need to. If they are able to move quickly around the court, the team players will be able to cover all areas of the court, which makes it more difficult for the opposing team to score points against them.

How can speed impact negatively on your performance?

If even one player within the volleyball team does not possess a high enough level of speed, then that player will be unable to move quickly enough around the court. This will consequently put additional pressure on the other players to cover areas of the court to compensate for that player. This can, therefore, result in gaps in the court, which the opposition can exploit to score more points.

 THINGS TO DO AND THINK ABOUT

1 Think of activities that you have covered in your course where speed played an important factor in the game/position/role that you had within the performance. Give some examples when it was helpful to possess good speed within this performance.

2 What would the impact have been had you not had good speed?

3 Choose a team sport. What are the positions/roles within this sport that require you to have a good level of speed?

 DON'T FORGET

Improving fitness improves how efficiently your heart works during performance, and also how quickly it recovers after performance.

VIDEO LINK

Watch the clip at www.brightredbooks.net/N5PE to see three examples of how to improve CRE.

 ONLINE TEST

Test how well you know this topic by taking the 'Physical factors' test online at www.brightredbooks.net/N5PE

PHYSICAL FACTORS 2

STRENGTH

Strength is the ability to exert a force on an object by using the muscles, which contract during the exertion of force. There are, however, three different types of strength that are important within different activities:

- Static strength
- Explosive strength
- Dynamic strength

Read up on the explanations of the different types of strength in the aspects of fitness impacting on performance section, p17.

How can strength impact positively on your performance?

VIDEO LINK

Watch the clip showing an effective rugby scrum at www.brightredbooks.net/N5PE

EXAMPLE STATIC STRENGTH

An example of how **static strength** can have a positive impact on performance is a rugby scrum. Static strength allows the scrum to hold a low, strong position prior to both teams engaging, and it prevents the other team from advancing forwards.

EXAMPLE DYNAMIC STRENGTH

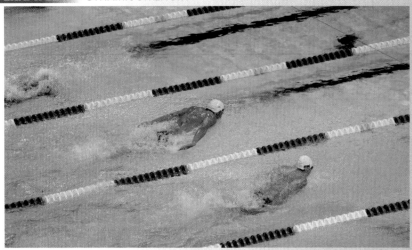

An example of how **dynamic strength** can have a positive impact on performance is in swimming. Michael Phelps is an American Olympic swimmer. He demonstrates excellent dynamic strength in his upper body. This helps propel him through the water at a much faster pace than the other competitors.

VIDEO LINK

Watch the video clip of the Olympic qualifying round of high jumping at www.brightredbooks.net/N5PE. You will see each jumper displaying excellent explosive strength.

EXAMPLE EXPLOSIVE STRENGTH

An example of how **explosive strength** can have a positive impact on performance is in high jumping. High jumpers require a high degree of explosive strength to help them drive their bodies upwards to clear the bar.

All three types of strength are required in almost every sport – some more so than others. It depends on the **nature** and **demands** of that chosen activity. In badminton, for example, dynamic strength is important as this allows you to keep hitting the shuttle to the back of the court with a sustained amount of power. This, in turn, forces your opponent to the back of the court and can make it difficult for them to return the shuttle in an attacking way.

contd

A long jumper requires explosive strength to allow them to jump further than their competitors, and a diver is required to have excellent static strength to allow them to hold their body in a straight position before they enter the water.

How can strength impact negatively on your performance?

If you don't have the required type of strength in your chosen activity, this can impact negatively in several ways on your performance. Here are two examples.

> **EXAMPLE**   TABLE TENNIS
>
> A table tennis player who does not possess enough dynamic strength would be unable to force their opponent away from the table and into a 'deep position'. Their opponent could exploit this weakness by attacking the areas where there was obvious space or by deliberately forcing the player to the back of the table where they will find it difficult to return the shot.

> **EXAMPLE**   BASKETBALL
>
> A lack of explosive strength in basketball can make it difficult to perform an effective jump shot. This will result in fewer 'three point' shots being taken and will force the player to drive in closer to the basket and shoot. However, if the defending team set up using zonal marking, this can become very difficult to penetrate.

DON'T FORGET

Different types of strength are needed for different sports, and even for different roles within team sports.

LOCAL MUSCULAR ENDURANCE (LME)

Local muscular endurance is the ability of a muscle (or group of muscles) to work continuously for a long time without tiring.

How can LME impact positively on your performance?

A rower requires a high level of local muscular endurance to perform effectively. Katherine Grainger won Olympic gold in the 2012 Olympics. The LME in her arms and legs enabled her and her team mate to maintain a consistent pace throughout the duration of the race.

How can LME impact negatively on your performance?

If Katherine Grainger and her team mate had possessed poor LME, the rhythm and speed at which they were rowing would have dropped to a much slower pace as fatigue began to set in. This would have resulted in the opposition catching them.

THINGS TO DO AND THINK ABOUT

1   Consider activities that you have covered within your course and find examples of static, explosive and dynamic strength.

2   What effect did each type of strength have on your performance? This can be positive or negative.

3   a   What tests could you use to measure LME?

    b   Can you describe in detail how you could carry out this test?

ONLINE TEST

Test how well you know this topic by taking the 'Physical factors' test online at www.brightredbooks.net/N5PE

SKILL-RELATED FACTORS 1

There are three main skill-related factors that impact on performance. These are:

- Agility
- Timing
- Reaction time

AGILITY

Agility is the ability to change the direction of the body in an efficient and effective manner. To achieve this, however, we must combine speed, balance and coordination. Individual sports such as badminton, tennis and squash all require a high level of agility. Similarly, agility is also important within team activities such as rugby, football, hockey and basketball.

How can agility impact positively on your performance?

EXAMPLE BASKETBALL

A 'small guard' in basketball has to move and change direction quickly as they move up the court. Their ability to move and change direction quickly in and out of the opposing team's defence allows them to drive and penetrate through the defence. These quick movements also mean that the defence are pulled out of position and, as a result, the 'small guard' creates gaps for their team to exploit. This results in greater goal-scoring opportunities.

How can agility impact negatively on your performance?

EXAMPLE BASKETBALL

If the 'point guard' within a basketball team does not possess agility, it becomes difficult for them to create goal-scoring opportunities, or to attack the basket. As it is their job to control the tempo of the game, it is important that they are agile and able to change direction and move the ball from one side of the court to the other.

DON'T FORGET

Agility is achieved by combining speed, balance and coordination.

TIMING

Timing is the ability to perform a skill, action or movement at exactly the right time within a performance. Aesthetic activities, such as gymnastics and dance, require a high level of timing to perform effectively. Timing is also important in activities such as high jump and golf. Timing is, in fact, a factor that is important in almost every activity.

VIDEO LINK

Watch the high jumper in slow motion at www. brightredbooks.net/N5PE

How can timing impact positively on your performance?

EXAMPLE HIGH JUMP

A high jumper requires a high level of timing as they approach the bar. During the very precise run-up, they need to decide at which point to drive their bodily force downwards to drive up their arms and legs to clear the bar. If the athlete is able to time this action well, they will be able to clear the height successfully.

How can timing impact negatively on your performance?

A defender in football who has a poor level of timing will miss tackles and, as a result, the opposition will have greater goal-scoring opportunities. A defender who mistimes headers in the 18-yard box is also in danger of allowing the opposition more chance at goal. This, in turn, puts more pressure on the goal keeper and other defenders within the team.

REACTION TIME

Reaction time is the ability to react quickly to stimuli. This could be in the form of a sound or something that you see or feel. A swimmer must react to the sound of the starter before beginning their race. A dancer will respond and react to the beat of the music.

How can reaction time impact positively on your performance?

It's an advantage to have good reactions within many activities.

> **EXAMPLE** SPRINT
>
> Usain Bolt had to have excellent reactions to enable him to win both the 100 m and 200 m at the Olympic Games in 2012. His excellent reactions allowed him to get out of the blocks quickly and into his stride before his competitors. Being able to react quickly to situations requires a high level of focus and concentration to allow you to shut out anything that might distract you.

VIDEO LINK

Watch the video of the swimmer Ryan Lochte starting his race at www. brightredbooks.net/N5PE

How can reaction time impact negatively on your performance?

There are a number of factors that can affect an individual's ability to react quickly. For example, an athlete who is very nervous or anxious will find it difficult to focus their attention solely on the sound of the starting gun and will be easily distracted by external sources such as the crowd. They might also be distracted by the fear of failure or negative thoughts.

In another example, when a free kick is awarded in football, the opposition must react quickly and get the relevant players behind the ball to defend. Failure to do so could lead to the ball being played quickly and a goal-scoring opportunity being created.

THINGS TO DO AND THINK ABOUT

1 Think of examples of sports/activities that you have covered in your course where agility plays an important role.

2 Can you describe a player/performer that you feel has good agility? Give examples.

3 What visible cues tell you that someone is calm before a performance?

4 Give examples of what you could do to calm yourself down before a performance and to focus your mind and emotions.

ONLINE TEST

Test how well you know this topic by taking the 'Skill-related factors' test online at www.brightredbooks.net/N5PE

SKILL-RELATED FACTORS 2

ASEPCTS OF SKILLS AND TECHNIQUES

In this section we will look at aspects of skills and techniques and how they can impact on your performance. These include:

- **Skill classification**
- Skilled performance
- **Stages of learning**

SKILL CLASSIFICATION

These tables identify the positive and negative impacts of different classifications of skills. Learn more about the classification of skills on p14.

	POSITIVE IMPACT
Simple skills	These are easy to perform with very little thought required. This allows you to focus your attention on other aspects of your performance.
Complex skills	The ability to perform complex skills allows you to adapt to any given situation. For example, if you are able to perform a tumble turn in swimming this will result in a faster time and winning more races.
Open skills	Performing open skills consistently allows you to cope much better with the external demands of your performance.
Closed skills	Practising a closed skill in a closed environment can be very beneficial, as it allows you to focus solely on the subroutines of the skill with very little movement or pressure. This is very useful at the **cognitive** stage of learning.

	NEGATIVE IMPACT
Simple skills	Depending on the situation, performing only simple skills can limit your performance and results. The inability to perform complex skills will affect confidence levels and motivation.
Complex skills	If you are unable to perform complex skills, you might find it particularly challenging when faced with an opponent who can. This, in turn, will put you under more pressure and could potentially result in you losing more points and games.
Open skills	You must be able to cope with the external demands of the performance to execute the skill well. Failure to do so will affect the performance in a negative way.
Closed skills	If a closed skill is practised in a closed environment for too long, progress will be limited. As a result, when you are placed in a competitive situation you will find it very difficult to perform this skill under pressure.

ONLINE

For more about the classification of skills, follow the link at www. brightredbooks.net/N5PE

SKILLED PERFORMANCE

A skilled performance is the ability to perform a wide repertoire of skills well in a pressurised situation. There will be skills within your game that come naturally to you and others that you will have to work hard at to improve. Being able to perform under pressure will positively impact on your performance because it will allow you to win more points, score more baskets, or whatever it is you do in your activity. Being unable to execute such skills consistently under pressure could result in you or your team losing the match.

STAGES OF LEARNING

There are three stages of learning: cognitive, practice and automatic.

How can the stages of learning impact positively on your performance?

If you use appropriate feedback to identify the stage of learning you are at, this will enable you to select an appropriate method of practice to improve your performance. You need different types of feedback to help you at different stages of learning. For example, someone at the cognitive stage will rely heavily on external feedback from a teacher or coach. This is because the performer has very limited knowledge at this stage of how to perform the skill correctly.

How can the stages of learning impact negatively on your performance?

If you don't consider the stages of learning, this can have several negative impacts on your performance. For example, if you are at the cognitive stage of learning with limited knowledge and understanding of how the skill should be performed and you create a practice that is too difficult and intense, then you are not going to improve and you will become demotivated as a result of a poor success rate. It is important that you select methods of practice that are appropriate for and relevant to the stage of learning.

DON'T FORGET

The stages of learning are covered in more detail on pp80–81 of this Study Guide.

ONLINE TEST

Test how well you know this topic by taking the 'Skill-related factors' test online at www.brightredbooks.net/N5PE

 THINGS TO DO AND THINK ABOUT

1   Consider the methods of practice that you have used to improve a skill.

2   Explain what method you used and why it was appropriate.

STRUCTURE, STRATEGY OR COMPOSITION 1

WHAT IS STRUCTURE, STRATEGY OR COMPOSITION?

A structure, strategy or composition is a plan of action that you as a team, or as an individual, plan on carrying out to perform effectively. Different sporting activities will have different structures, strategies or compositions, depending on a number of factors.

EXAMPLE STRUCTURE: 3–5–2 FORMATION IN HOCKEY

A hockey team might use a 3–5–2 structure to allow the team to control the midfield area of the pitch, and also to use the wide right and left midfielders to create **width in attack** by pushing them further up the pitch to support the two strikers. Having these wide players in this position also allows them to drop back and help the three defenders. By dominating the midfield area, the five midfielders act as a strong first line of defence, which would be difficult to breakdown and penetrate, and dictate the tempo of the game.

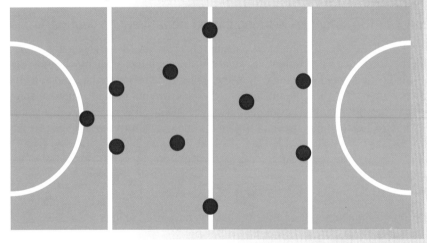

ONLINE

Follow the link at www.brightredbooks.net/N5PE to read more about running strategies.

EXAMPLE STRATEGY: 800 m RUNNER

A strategy that could be used within 800 m running would be to stay tucked in behind the leading runner on the windy parts of the track. By doing so, you can use their slipstream and conserve energy because the leading runner is having to work harder against the resistance of the wind, and will therefore use more energy. Towards the end of the race, you can then move out from behind them and begin sprinting towards the finish line.

EXAMPLE COMPOSITION: RHYTHMIC GYMNASTS

Rhythmic gymnasts use music and movement to tell a story to their audience. To get their message across, they give careful consideration to the music that they have chosen and the types of movement that they incorporate into their routine.

contd

 **ACTIVITY:**

1 Within the activities that you have covered in your course, think of a structure, strategy or composition that you have used.

2 Draw a diagram of this and describe it in as much detail as possible.

3 Explain why you used this structure, strategy or composition. Consider the strengths and weaknesses within your team.

DECIDING ON A STRUCTURE, STRATEGY OR COMPOSITION

Often the structure, strategy or composition that you choose to use will depend on a number of key factors, including:

- your own skills and qualities
- your team's skills and qualities
- the strengths and weaknesses of the opposition
- the circumstances
- your own roles and responsibilities
- your team's roles and responsibilities.

Before you decide on what structure, strategy or composition you are going to use, you must be aware of your own (and your team's) personal skills and qualities – often referred to as strengths and weaknesses. If the structure, strategy or composition that you choose is based on these, then you will increase your chances of a successful performance.

You also need to consider the strengths and weaknesses of the opposition. This ensures that you can capitalise on and exploit any weakness in the opposition's game, as well as being aware of their strengths.

The structure, strategy or composition that you choose might also be influenced by what is at stake. If, for example, a football team are winning by a narrow margin in the latter stages of a cup competition, they might choose to play more defensively to maintain their lead.

It is vital that every member of the team is aware of their role within the chosen structure, strategy or composition. For example, a netball player in the position of centre must fully understand that their role is a very demanding one, and that the tempo at which the game will be played is often dictated by them. They must have excellent levels of CRE to allow them to move up and down the court to support in attack and in defence. If this player is not aware of their roles and responsibilities, then it will become increasingly difficult for their team to get the ball up the court quickly to create goal-scoring opportunities.

 DON'T FORGET

If a performer is ignorant of their strategy or their role within the structure, then they are unlikely to succeed in their performance.

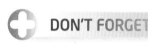 **ONLINE TEST**

Test how well you know this topic by taking the 'Structure, strategy or composition' test online at www.brightredbooks.net/ N5PE

 THINGS TO DO AND THINK ABOUT

1 Think of the roles and responsibilities that you have carried out throughout your course. Give some examples of these roles and responsibilities and how they helped your team/performance.

2 A football team initially opt for a very attack-minded structure (3–5–2) as they set out to win the first leg of their important cup match. However, as the game progresses and the score line is 1–1, they lose their central defender to injury and do not have a like-for-like replacement on the bench. There is 25 minutes left on the clock.

Consider this scenario and, in groups of two to three, come up with a plan of action for the football team.

Think about all the possibilities before deciding on the best plan of action.

STRUCTURE, STRATEGY OR COMPOSITION 2

PRINCIPLES OF PLAY

Within any structure, it is important that you are aware of the Principles of Play and the impact that they can have on your performance. The Principles of Play are split into attack and defence.

Attack

1 **Penetration**

When a team is on the attack, it is important that they are able to penetrate the opposition's defence. By doing so, they have an increased chance of creating a goal-scoring opportunity. The team must figure out the most effective way of penetrating the defence, whether it be by playing a long ball over the top of the defence and into the space behind, or by drawing the defence out of position, which will create gaps for the ball to be played through.

2 **Depth**

A team that has **depth in attack** can make it very difficult for the opposing team to get the ball effectively out of defence and relieve the pressure, both on them and on their goal keeper. This Principle of Play also increases the team's chance of creating another attacking situation very quickly.

3 **Width**

Width in attack allows the ball to be played to the wide areas of the pitch, which in turn draws the opposing team's defenders out wide. This then creates gaps and space for the ball to be passed through.

4 **Mobility**

A team that demonstrates good mobility will show a varied pace of play and good movement on and off the ball. This will make it very difficult for the opposition to mark and defend.

5 **Support**

Players need to make themselves available in an attacking situation to maintain the pressure on the opposition.

Defence

1 **Delay**

Teams need to slow the opposing team down when they are attacking. This can be achieved by putting a player under pressure, forcing them to make decisions too quickly and, therefore, creating a context where it's easier for them to make a mistake. Delaying the opposition's attack also allows players in your team enough time to track back and get into position.

2 **Support**

Players must support surrounding players when the opposition are on the attack by offering passing options.

COMPOSITION

With dance and gymnastics, the performer must consider the compositional elements of their performance. For example, in gymnastics the routine or sequence will be built around a series of movements that flow effortlessly and link well together. A rhythmic gymnast might use music or other equipment to add to the complexity of the routine.

The main principles to be considered when composing a routine or sequence are:

- Levels
- Space
- Flow
- Dynamics

Levels

The routine should incorporate high, medium and low levels throughout. Demonstrating such changes in height throughout the routine allows the performer to display a wide repertoire of simple and complex skills.

Space

Moving from one side of the mats or hall to the other allows the performer to think creatively and more imaginatively, which can add to the excitement of the routine.

Flow

Allowing the routine to flow seamlessly from one skill to the next will result in the performer scoring a higher mark from the judges, because the transitions are much smoother.

Dynamics

The ability to change the speed and direction at which the performer is moving can add to the intensity and excitement within the overall performance. The performer can also use dynamics to tell a story through their performance.

Compositions are usually set ahead of time and are carried out as planned.

ONLINE TEST

Test how well you know this topic by taking the 'Structure, strategy or composition' test online at www.brightredbooks.net/N5PE

 THINGS TO DO AND THINK ABOUT

Watch the Women's Floor Exercise Final from the London 2012 Olympics at www.brightredbooks.net/N5PE and identify the use of levels, space, flow and dynamics in each performance.

MENTAL AND EMOTIONAL FACTORS 1

MENTAL FACTORS: AN OVERVIEW

Mental factors that can have an impact on performance include:

- Level of arousal and motivation
- Concentration
- Information processing
- Decision-making
- Problem-solving
- Attention span
- Focus of attention
- Mental toughness
- Movement anticipation
- Due recognition
- Perception

LEVEL OF AROUSAL AND MOTIVATION

As we learned in the first chapter, arousal is your level of excitement, motivation and readiness to perform. Your level of arousal must be optimal for your performance. Over-excitement or stress (high levels of arousal) can be just as detrimental to your performance as fatigue, complacency or lack of interest (low arousal).

Levels of arousal differ from athlete to athlete and between sports. The nature of a sport may have an impact on the optimal level of arousal required. For example, some sports require a performer to remain calm and composed over a long period of time, whereas in other sports a performer requires a high level of arousal in short bursts. As a general rule, complex skills in competitive situations usually require a low level of arousal. In contrast, simple tasks done during training require a higher level of arousal.

If your level of arousal is not at its optimum, there are techniques you can use to increase or decrease it. Your arousal level can be increased by an active warm-up or by listening to music or a motivational speech or team talk. If your arousal level is too high, you can use relaxation techniques, visualisation or listening to music to help you relax.

How level of arousal can impact on your performance

When your level of arousal is at its optimum, you will feel ready to perform and your ability to cope under pressure will increase.

DON'T FORGET

Consider the optimal level of arousal needed for your particular performance. This could be high or low depending on the nature of your chosen activity.

EXAMPLE   HIGH AROUSAL LEVEL: RUGBY

Before a game of rugby, players usually listen to music which will help them focus and raise their level of arousal. Players will then take part in an active warm-up before the match to get their bodies ready and focus their minds on the match ahead. Just before the match, the coach will then give the players a team talk to raise their level of arousal even further before the match starts. This means that by the time the game kicks off, players should have reached their optimal level of arousal and should feel completely ready for the match.

Rugby is a very physical game which requires aggression and physicality. Due to the nature of rugby, players are required to have a high level of arousal.

contd

EXAMPLE   LOW AROUSAL LEVEL: GOLF

By contrast, golf is a game that requires a high level of accuracy and players must stay calm under pressure, so they need a lower level of arousal. This means that players must often find a way to deal with nerves and anxiety. Before, and during, a round of golf, players will use techniques such as visualisation and controlled breathing to calm themselves down.

CONCENTRATION

In sports, concentration is the ability to completely focus your attention on a task for a period of time. Concentration is considered to be one of the main mental factors required for a successful performance. Some sports require intense concentration for short bursts of time, whereas other sports require a performer to remain focused over prolonged periods.

Losing focus during a performance will often result in a higher frequency of mistakes, decrease in accuracy, decreased work rate and, eventually, demotivation. The most common types of distraction to concentration are anxiety, mistakes, fatigue, weather, opponents and negative thoughts.

How concentration can impact on your performance

EXAMPLE   CONCENTRATION OVER PROLONGED PERIODS: TENNIS

Tennis is a sport that demands a lot of concentration from competitors. Matches can often last between two to three hours, and to be able to maintain a high performance level performers have to remain focused throughout the rallies. Before a match, competitors use different techniques to focus their minds and ensure that they concentrate. In between games, players are given drink breaks. During this time, you might see some competitors talking to themselves – this is called 'self-talk'. This technique is used by many performers to refocus their mind if they feel they are losing concentration during competitions. Loss of concentration for a tennis player can result in an increase in mistakes, increased frustration and a decrease in accuracy.

EXAMPLE   SHORT BURSTS OF INTENSE CONCENTRATION: DIVING

By contrast, diving requires short bursts of intense concentration. Competitors are required to execute a dive with a high level of difficulty and accuracy. Before their dive, a performer will focus on the subroutines of their dive and during execution they will concentrate on every movement. A slight loss of concentration could result in a small error (which could impact on their score) or in a bigger error (which may result in injury).

 VIDEO LINK

Watch the video at www. brightredbooks.net/N5PE of Andy Murray and Novak Djokovic playing tennis. During this long rally, concentration plays a major factor. Each player must remain focused, even as they start to fatigue.

 VIDEO LINK

Watch the video at www. brightredbooks.net/N5PE which demonstrates the intense concentration required to be a successful diver.

 THINGS TO DO AND THINK ABOUT

Consider sports that you have taken part in. Describe ways in which you have raised/ lowered your level of arousal.

 ONLINE TEST

Test how well you know this topic by taking the 'Mental and emotional factors' test online at www. brightredbooks.net/N5PE

MENTAL AND EMOTIONAL FACTORS 2

INFORMATION PROCESSING

Information processing is the ability to separate essential and non-essential information during a performance. The speed at which a performer can process information usually depends on the nature of the skill being performed, the environment the performance is taking place in and the performer's experience. Initially, a performer might take some time to process information, resulting in slower decision-making and a higher frequency of mistakes. However, as a performer becomes more experienced, the decision-making process will become quicker and subsequent decisions will be more precise.

How information processing can impact on your performance

> **EXAMPLE**   VOLLEYBALL
>
> When the ball is served in volleyball, the receiving team must quickly process information to be able to set up an attacking move. The receiving player must take into consideration the flight of the ball and where their team mates are. Fast information processing will result in the correct shot being played, whereas poor, or slow, information processing will result in poor execution or failure to reach the ball.

DECISION-MAKING

Information processing and decision-making are closely linked. Many decisions in sport are a direct result of your brain processing information in seconds. These decisions take place during performances and are a result of the environment around you constantly changing. However, decision-making can also take place before a performance, when a performer might make a choice based on prior knowledge or the demands of their sport.

How decision-making can impact on your performance

> **EXAMPLE**   FOOTBALL
>
> Football is an open sport, played in an ever-changing environment.
>
> Before a match, a coach might make a decision to play a certain formation – for example, 4–4–2. This type of decision has been made prior to a performance and means that the team has a basic structure to work from during the game. The coach will have made this decision based on the:
> - strengths of their own players and/or
> - weaknesses or formation of the other team.
>
> During the game, players will also be required to make many decisions. If players create enough space and time, they will have more time for the decision-making process, therefore increasing the accuracy of their skill execution. However, as the pressure increases, the demands on the time they have for the decision-making process will also increase, and they will therefore be more likely to make mistakes.

EMOTIONAL FACTORS: AN OVERVIEW

Emotions play a big factor in performance and enjoyment of sport. Emotional factors that can have an impact on performance – positively and negatively – include:

- **happiness** and **sadness**
- anger
- fear and anxiety.

Happiness and sadness

Basic feelings such as happiness or sadness before or during a performance can have a big impact on your overall approach and outlook. Feeling happy before a performance will mean that you approach a performance with optimism and increased self-confidence. Approaching a performance with a higher level of self-confidence should result in a fewer number of errors and feeling less anxious under pressure.

By contrast, feeling sad before a performance will have a negative effect. Feeling sad or low can result in self-doubt or a negative mind set. Lower self-confidence will be detrimental to performance.

Anger

Certain sports require some level of aggression – for example, contact sports such as lacrosse or rugby. By using a form of controlled aggression, players can gain a physical and mental advantage over their opponents. However, if channelled incorrectly, aggression can present itself as frustration or anger. If anger is uncontrolled, it can be very detrimental to performance. When angry, a performer's decision-making, self-control and skill level can all be affected. In sport, anger can display itself in many forms – for example, at a basic level performers can become frustrated with themselves or others. This kind of frustration usually impacts negatively on an individual's performance, causing them to make poor decisions and more errors. In some cases, anger can lead to loss of self-control.

Fear and anxiety

Anxiety, or dealing with stress, affects performers in different ways. For some, anxiety can be detrimental to their performance because it can cause stress, self-doubt and even panic under pressure. In these cases, the performer's decision-making will be affected, which will lead to mistakes or underperforming.

For others, a certain amount of anxiety can have a positive effect on their performance. Anxiety can cause some performers to focus more and raise their performance.

Too much anxiety or stress, however, will always have a negative effect. There are different ways in which you can deal with anxiety – for example, listening to music to calm you down, mentally rehearsing your routine or role within your performance, visualising different situations, set pieces or routines, or positive self-talk.

 THINGS TO DO AND THINK ABOUT

Think about an activity you have performed in recently. Consider any emotional factors that affected you prior to that performance. How do you think your emotions impacted on your performance? Is this something you can improve on or repeat in the future?

 DON'T FORGET

Although a certain amount of stress or anxiety can benefit some athletes, too much will never have a positive effect on your performance.

 VIDEO LINK

Check out the 'Self-Talk' clip at www.brightredbooks. net/N5PE for tips on how to master positive self-talk.

 ONLINE TEST

Test how well you know this topic by taking the 'Mental and emotional factors' test online at www. brightredbooks.net/N5PE

PHYSIOLOGICAL AND MEDICAL FACTORS

OVERVIEW

These are factors that can affect you physically. They will affect your body and will possibly have a negative impact on your performance. It's important to note that an illness is often something which is only temporary, whereas a medical condition could be something that a performer has to cope with permanently. If they are taking some sort of medicine or receiving some sort of treatment, it will affect how well they perform – even if it does not stop them taking part altogether.

Listed below are some physiological and medical factors that can have a negative effect on performance.

FATIGUE

Fatigue has a negative impact on performance. It occurs when the body (or parts of the body) gets so tired that it stops working properly. This can often be a result of over-training and not allowing the body sufficient time to recover properly. When the body is fatigued, the performer's skill level drops, they begin to make mistakes and self-doubt can kick in, resulting in a downward psychological spiral.

Fatigue can also result in more injuries occurring, due to the performer's inability to carry out movements properly. Their technique will also begin to suffer as a result.

If fatigue has really set in, the only solution is for the performer to stop before they do any further damage, either physically and psychologically. It is also important that coaches and managers can recognise the signs of fatigue and intervene at the earliest point possible.

ONLINE

Check out ten inspirational athletes with asthma at www.brightredbooks.net/N5PE

VIDEO LINK

Find out about one athlete's experience of asthma by watching the video at www.brightredbooks.net/N5PE

DON'T FORGET

Illnesses are often just temporary, whereas medical conditions can be something that a performer has to cope with permanently.

ASTHMA

Asthma is a disease that causes difficulty in breathing. It can be brought about by allergies, infections or even emotional situations. It causes involuntary contraction of the **bronchioles**, which makes the sufferer wheeze and struggle for breath.

Asthma can be controlled by drugs and medicines (the most common of which is an inhalant spray) but an asthma sufferer might find endurance events more challenging than a non-asthma sufferer.

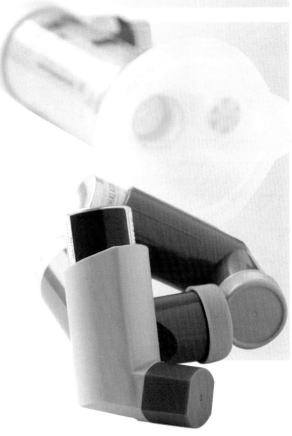

HAYFEVER

Hayfever affects the respiratory system. It is caused by an allergy to pollen, usually from trees and grass. It causes an inflammation of the membranes in the nose, which makes the sufferer sneeze and their eyes water. It only usually affects people in spring and summer when the pollen count is high. There are medications available to relieve the condition, but many of these can cause drowsiness, which may affect the athlete.

COLDS AND FLU

Colds and flu are infectious diseases that can be passed from one person to another. As the athlete's body tries to fight the infection, this often results in low energy levels, which in turn make it difficult for the athlete to train effectively. It can also be dangerous to train when the athlete is trying to overcome an infection.

ONLINE TEST

Test how well you know this topic by taking the 'Physiological and medical factors' test online at www.brightredbooks.net/N5PE

LACK OF SLEEP

Nervous energy or anxiety before a major event can lead to sleepless nights, and tiredness can have a very negative impact on performance because it can lead to reduced levels of concentration and coordination. The athlete's movements can also become less efficient.

OVERTRAINING

Overtraining can lead to overexertion, fatigue and inconsistent performances. In many physical activities now, there are opportunities to play all year round instead of just through a traditional season, so it is easier to overdo it. The pressure is on performers to continually improve: as a result, they are reluctant to take sufficient rest periods throughout the season.

THINGS TO DO AND THINK ABOUT

List the signs of fatigue. Choose an activity of your choice and describe how fatigue could affect a performer.

ONLINE

Learn more about over-training by following the link at www.brightredbooks.net/N5PE

PSYCHOLOGICAL, NUTRITIONAL AND DIETARY FACTORS

PSYCHOLOGICAL FACTORS

Until recently, performers and coaches have tended to focus on the physical factors that impact positively and negatively on performances. However, the psychological factors that impact on performances are now recognised as being just as important, and are being investigated more closely. The professional golfer Tiger Woods speaks openly about the importance of being mentally strong and prepared for every tournament that he plays in:

'My mindset is my biggest asset. I expect to win every tournament I play.'

Tiger Woods (Silent Mind Golf, *Robin Sieger 2010*)

The following psychological factors impact on performance:

- Tension
- Anxiety
- Boredom
- Pressure
- Motivation
- Self-talk and mental rehearsal

Tension

Tension can have a positive or negative effect on your performance. It is how you manage this tension that determines the type of effect it has. You might have heard the expression that he or she 'choked under pressure'. A recent example of a sportsman who choked under pressure was Adam Scott the golfer. He began his final round of 'The Open Championships' with a four-stroke lead, but made a series of very simple errors on each of the last four holes, which resulted in him eventually losing out to Ernie Els.

Anxiety

DON'T FORGET

Psychological factors that impact on performance are often overlooked by athletes and coaches, but it is just as important to consider these as it is to monitor physical factors!

Anxiety can also have a positive and negative effect on an individual's performance. For example, as an athlete prepares for an event, their body naturally produces adrenaline. This can often lead to an improved or enhanced performance. However, if the athlete becomes over-anxious or nervous, their performance can suffer. The main reason that individuals get nervous prior to a performance is due to a fear of failure or of letting someone down if they do not perform well. This is summed up by the famous American baseball player Babe Ruth:

'Never let the fear of striking out get in your way.'

Boredom

If an individual is bored when they are training or performing, it is unlikely that they will perform to their full potential. If training sessions are not stimulating and challenging enough, then it is likely that boredom will set in. Boredom can have an even greater impact on performance within team activities. For example, if a team is being heavily beaten, some of the team members might 'switch off' and show a lack of interest in the game.

Pressure

Individuals and teams are always trying to put their opponents under pressure by the way that they play the game. If they find a weakness, they will try to exploit it. To be successful, it is vital for a player to be able to keep going under pressure. This is what is meant by 'soaking up the pressure'.

contd

Motivation

You need motivation to develop and continue to improve your performance. Motivation can come from a variety of sources. Some sportspeople are motivated by extrinsic factors such as money, reputation and lifestyle. Others, however, are intrinsically motivated. **Intrinsic motivation** is an individual's personal desire to improve and be the best sportsperson that they can be.

Self-talk and mental rehearsal

Self-talk and mental rehearsal is an important part of an athlete's preparation prior to an event. The athlete uses visualisation techniques by imagining what they plan to do during their performance. For example, Usain Bolt uses visualisation techniques as he plans in his mind how he is going to start his race, how he is going to run it, how he is going to finish and what his posture is going to be like. He is mentally running the race in his mind. Positive self-talk usually consists of positive words or phrases which inspire or motivate us, or remind us to focus on the task.

NUTRITIONAL AND DIETARY FACTORS

An individual's diet can have both a positive and negative impact on performance. People participating in different sports or activities will require different diets depending on the demands and nature of the activity. Individuals who perform in activities that require a high level of sustained physical exertion to perform well will require a higher intake of carbohydrates.

Performers also need to be aware of what they eat **before**, **during** and **after** the activity. This is paramount if the individual is to perform at his or her best in this activity and the next.

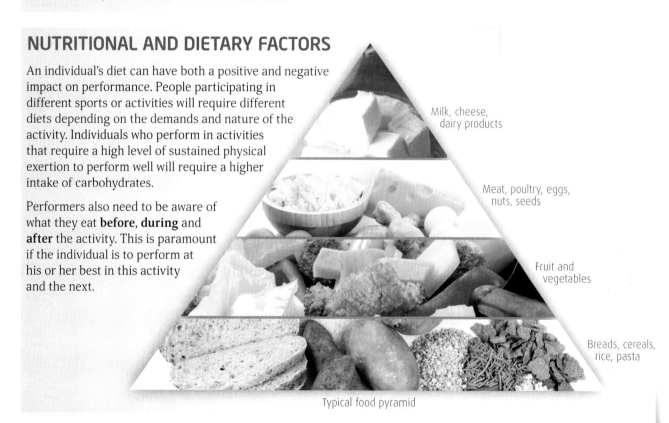

Milk, cheese, dairy products

Meat, poultry, eggs, nuts, seeds

Fruit and vegetables

Breads, cereals, rice, pasta

Typical food pyramid

 THINGS TO DO AND THINK ABOUT

1 Think of a particular event or performance where you have felt very anxious and nervous beforehand.

    a What caused you to feel this way?

    b How did you perform that day? Do you think that your nerves played a part in your performance?

    c What would you have done differently if you could go back?

2 Discuss ways of managing your anxiety levels with a partner.

3 Think of foods that athletes eat regularly. Now consider your own activity or sport. What types of food should you eat before a performance, and why? What types of food should you eat after a performance, and why?

 ONLINE

Find out more about eating a healthy and balanced diet by following the link at www.brightredbooks.net/N5PE

 ONLINE TEST

Take the 'Psychological, nutritional and dietary factors' test at www.brightredbooks.net/N5PE

SOCIAL FACTORS

SOCIAL FACTORS

There are many social factors that can dictate how well an individual or team will perform. These factors can impact both positively or negatively. We will now look at the following aspects and how they can influence performance:

- Roles and responsibilities
- Social groupings
- Inclusion
- Etiquette
- Cooperation

Roles and responsibilities

Our decision to participate in a particular activity is often dependant on a number of factors such as whether our friends or family have participated in it, whether it is competitive or non-competitive, or whether it is team or individual. Our opinions are often shaped by others around us.

The roles and responsibilities that we are given within our chosen activity can be another reason why we often choose to pursue one sport over another. The table below shows some of the different roles that people play within various sporting activities and the benefits that these roles can have on you and others.

ROLE	BENEFIT TO YOU	BENEFIT TO OTHERS
Performer	Enjoyment, satisfaction, achievement	Provides satisfaction – people enjoy sharing your success
Coach	Improves self-confidence, gains coaching qualifications	Improves athletes' physical, mental and emotional performance
Captain	Leadership and **communication** skills are developed	Helps the coaching staff
Choreographer	Outlet for aesthetic creativity	Provides exciting and challenging context for dancers

 **ACTIVITY**

Think of a sport that you participate in. What roles and responsibilities are people involved in?

Social groupings

Social groupings in your personal life are the groups to which you are attached because of circumstances and choice. These social groupings can either have a positive or negative influence on your involvement in sport. Friendships and relationships within sports teams can, however, become quite complex. Strong personalities within teams can affect the team in both positive and negative ways. It is the team captain's role to try to tap into everyone's individual strengths and use them in the best way possible.

Inclusion

Everyone – regardless of their age, gender, social status or ability – should have the opportunity to participate in any sporting activity. It is the responsibility of the authorities to ensure that everyone has access to the facilities within schools and sporting venues, regardless of their capabilities.

If opportunities and facilities are limited, then inclusion just won't happen. A person who is wheelchair-bound and wants to learn to play tennis must have easy access to and from the building, usually in the form of a ramp. If this is not in place, it makes it very difficult for that person to pursue their sporting interests.

contd

DON'T FORGET

The team captain's job is to try to tap into everyone's individual strengths and use them in the best way possible.

Etiquette

Etiquette, leadership, teamwork responsibility and respect all play an important role within sport. Etiquette is about conducting ourselves in a sporting manner. This is often referred to as 'the unwritten rules' of the sport. For example, at the end of a tennis match, regardless of the outcome, the players will usually meet at the net and shake hands with one another and then with the umpire. Or if a player is fouled during a football match, a member of the opposition usually helps him back up onto his feet.

A person demonstrating good etiquette before, during and after a performance ensures that the game has been carried out fairly. It is therefore less likely that poor behaviour and bad temper will occur afterwards.

Poor etiquette can also have a negative impact on your performance and on that of others around you. For example, you will have seen incidents when a decision goes against a player, and they either pick up the ball and throw it away, argue with the referee, their teammates or the opposition, or even use bad language. These are usually signs that their performance is deteriorating because they are letting their frustration about the decision get to them, and they lose focus. They also make the people around them lose focus.

Cooperation

Cooperation is vitally important to every team activity. Everyone within the team needs to feel valued, confident and able to express themselves without fear of what team mates might say. Teams that display excellent cooperation skills are usually the teams that perform well. FC Barcelona, for example, plays some of the best football in the world. This is due to the fact that they cooperate well together: they have a **trust** in each other's ability which allows them to play with confidence and fluency.

Teams or groups that do not cooperate well often perform poorly. Players are often reluctant to take risks because they are worried that their team mates will get angry with them. This results in the players feeling limited in what they can do. A player who is very creative, for example, might feel restricted by team mates who are not supportive and who do not cooperate effectively as part of the team or group.

VIDEO LINK

See an example of this by watching the clip 'FC Barcelona: 42 Passes, 1 Goal' at www.brightredbooks.net/N5PE

THINGS TO DO AND THINK ABOUT

1   The next time you are visiting a sports centre, look around and see how inclusive the facility is. Is there a ramp or lift? Are the door frames wide enough for wheelchair access?

2   Can you give some examples of how you would ensure that everyone within your team was included and felt valued?

3   Complete the table below. It looks at the positive and negative impacts that social groupings can have on your involvement in sport.

SOCIAL GROUPINGS	POSITIVE EFFECT	NEGATIVE EFFECT
Peers	If they enjoy and play sport, you will join in.	If they do not share your interest, they might try to encourage you to give up the sport. Peer pressure.
Family		
Gender		
Race		
Socio-economic		

ONLINE TEST

Test how well you know this topic by taking the 'Social factors' test online at www.brightredbooks.net/N5PE

DESIGNING A PERSONAL DEVELOPMENT PLAN

This chapter covers the following Outcome and Assessment Standards for the Physical Education: Developing Personal Performance (National 5) Unit:

Outcome 2: Develop personal performance in physical activities by:

2.1 Describing strengths and areas for development in a performance

2.2 Preparing and implementing a personal development plan containing clearly identified development targets

2.3 Selecting and applying two approaches to impact positively on a performance

2.4 Monitoring and recording performance development sessions

OVERVIEW

You have to consider a number of factors when you are designing a personal development plan. What factors do you want to improve? What phase of training are you in? What are you trying to achieve by the end of the plan? How are you going to achieve these goals?

DESCRIBING STRENGTHS AND AREAS FOR DEVELOPMENT

ONLINE

Follow the link at www. brightredbooks.net/N5PE for a useful website about planning.

To be able to develop your personal development plan, you need first of all to use the information you have gathered about your performance to identify your areas for development. For example, if you are a 1500m runner and you want to improve your performance, you should gather your initial data by running a 1500m race and recording your time. You should then consider the key aspects of fitness required to run a fast 1500m. If you carry out appropriate standardised tests and identify that CRE is a weakness, then your areas for development should include a method of training that improves CRE.

You also need to think about the events/races that you are hoping to compete in. Your training should taper as a major competition gets closer, otherwise overtraining could result in injury, fatigue and poor performance. You need to go into the event in the best possible physical condition and have a strong, positive mindset. Setting short- and long-term goals over the course of the season will also help you stay motivated to train and improve.

SETTING CLEARLY IDENTIFIED TARGETS

Once you have identified your areas for development, you need to set clearly identified targets. You, therefore, need to monitor your performance after each training session to keep track of whether you have met these targets. You should also keep a record of any injuries that you might have picked up while training or during the season, because it is important to factor in that reversibility will occur. This will also help you to identify whether particular types of training have contributed to the injury.

ASPECTS OF FITNESS

If you are planning on developing an aspect or aspects of fitness, you will need to link the data you collected from **standardised tests** with **principles and methods of training**. This will help you to design a personal development plan that is specific to your needs and focuses on developing specific aspects of fitness.

SKILLS AND TECHNIQUE EXECUTION

If you are planning on developing specific skills or techniques within your chosen activity, you will need to link the data you collected about your performance (for example, **video analysis**, **observation schedules** or comparisons to a **model performer**) with **methods of practice**. This will help you to identify the specific skills and techniques you need to improve, and your **stage of skill learning**.

STRUCTURES, STRATEGIES AND COMPOSITION

If you are planning on developing your structure or strategy, you will need to link the data you collected from your performance (for example, from **match analysis** or **knowledge of results**) with ways of developing problem-solving and decision-making in games. The same applies if you are developing your team's structure or strategy.

Once you have identified your areas for development and set clearly identified targets, you can start to look in more depth at identifying phases of training, setting goals and keeping track of your training.

PRINCIPLES OF TRAINING

When you are setting your targets, you need to think about the following Principles of Training.

Progressive overload

The training programme must be progressive (become more difficult each week) if your performance is to improve.

Frequency

Frequency means the number of times per week that you are going to train. For example, you might set a target of increasing the frequency of your training from three to four times a week.

Intensity

Intensity means how hard you train. You can monitor this using a heart rate monitor to ensure that you are working within your training zone.

Duration

Duration is how long you train for. For example, you might set a target of increasing the duration of your continuous run from 25 minutes to 30 minutes.

 DON'T FORGET

Training methods must be **specific** to the aspect of area of your performance that you are trying to improve. Your training must also be **specific to the activity or sport** that you are participating in. Training must also be **specific to your own level of fitness**.

 VIDEO LINK

Watch the 'Principles of Training' video at www.brightredbooks.net/N5PE

 ONLINE TEST

Test how well you know this topic by taking the 'Designing a personal development plan' test online at www.brightredbooks.net/N5PE

 THINGS TO DO AND THINK ABOUT

1. What are the first things that you should do before creating a personal development plan?

2. What are the most effective methods of gathering data on your own performance and why were they effective?

3. What other factors must you consider before you can implement your personal development plan?

4. How do you plan to overcome any impacting factors throughout your personal development plan?

5. Look at all of the points that you need to consider before, during and after the personal development plan has been completed.

PHASES OF TRAINING

The type, intensity, frequency and duration of training will vary, depending on which phase you are at in your activity. For example, you would avoid doing a lot of exercise if you have a big competition the next day. It therefore makes sense to break your activity's season or calendar into three phases. These are:

- Preparation phase (pre-season)
- Competition phase (during the season)
- Transition phase (off-season)

The next few pages outline the key features of each phase, and the goal you are trying to achieve during each phase.

PREPARATION PHASE (PRE-SEASON)

Key features

- Training starts with general fitness work – there will usually be an initial focus on developing physical fitness.
- Specific skill drills and practices will be incorporated over time.
- Intensity is increased over time by shortening breaks, increasing work load and working for longer periods of time.
- During this phase, your programme should be specific to the nature of your activity and your role within that activity.

Your goal during this phase:

- To prepare your body and mind as best you can for the competition phase – you will benefit from the preparation phase when it comes to the competition phase.

VIDEO LINK

Watch the 'Nike Academy – Pre-Season Training' video at www.brightredbooks.net/ N5PE

> **EXAMPLE** RUGBY
>
> In the preparation phase, rugby teams focus initially on developing strength and size through weight training.
>
> As pre-season progresses, ball handling and contact drills will be introduced, and the focus from strength and size will shift to speed and cardio-respiratory endurance.
>
> Some aspects of the preparation phase will be the same for the whole team – for example, developing CRE. However, other aspects of the preparation phase will vary according to position.
>
> A winger is required to have good hands and to be very fast. Therefore, a large proportion of their preparation will focus more on ball-handling and speed work.
>
> By comparison, a second row is required to be bigger and stronger and have the ability to compete in the line-outs. They might, therefore, concentrate more on weight training and line-out work.

ONLINE

Check out the example about pre-season rugby at www. brightredbooks.net/N5PE

COMPETITION PHASE (DURING THE SEASON)

ONLINE

Head to www. brightredbooks.net/N5PE and check out the 'Competition Phase-Tennis' example.

Key features

- Training is 'tapered' towards competition and matches. This means training might become less intense, or the duration might decrease close to competitions to avoid injury and fatigue.
- Athletes are given time prior to a competition to mentally prepare.
- Athletes avoid situations where a competition is followed closely by high intensity exercise to give their body optimal time to rest and recover.

contd

Your goal during this phase:

- To maintain your skill-related fitness and physical fitness levels at their peak for competitions.

> ### EXAMPLE   DISTANCE RUNNER
>
> Following on from an intense preparation phase, a 5000 m runner will taper their training to avoid overtraining and fatigue.
>
> During the competition phase, the athlete will decrease the amount of times they train a week and will avoid intense training the day before an event. During this phase a 5000 m runner might choose to develop specific areas of their event – for example, they might work on their speed to help their sprint finish.
>
> A 5000 m runner will avoid intense exercise the day after a competition to give their body time to rest and recover.

TRANSITION PHASE (OFF-SEASON)

Key features

- This is the phase of training that takes place after the competition phase and before the next preparation phase.
- During this phase, athletes usually try to avoid competitions.
- Training is usually in the form of 'active rest' – for example, light jogging, cycling or swimming. This helps maintain a good level of general fitness.

Your goal during this phase:

- This phase is essential because it allows you to completely rest your body and make it ready for the preparation phase again.

> ### EXAMPLE   FOOTBALL
>
> A football season is long and puts a lot of stress on the body. Following the football season, players move into a transition phase.
>
> During this phase, players will allow their bodies a prolonged rest. They will probably participate in light exercise such as jogging, cycling or swimming, and will avoid intense exercise and competition.
>
> This ensures that when the players return for the pre-season or the preparation phase, their bodies are rested and ready to return to intense exercise without risk of fatigue-related injury.

 THINGS TO DO AND THINK ABOUT

Think of a sport/activity that you participate in and consider the type of training that you plan on carrying out at each of the three phases. Give some examples of training sessions that you might include.

	SPORT/ ACTIVITY	CONSIDER WHAT TYPE OF TRAINING YOU WOULD CARRY OUT IN THIS PHASE
Preparation phase		
Competition phase		
Transition phase		

 ONLINE

For more on the transition phase head to www. brightredbooks.net/N5PE

 DON'T FORGET

It is important to consider the phases of training. These will depend on what sport/activity you participate in and when your playing season begins and ends. When planning your personal development plan, you must take the phases of training into consideration.

 ONLINE TEST

Take the 'Phases of training' test online to check how much you know at www. brightredbooks.net/N5PE

GOAL SETTING

When you are planning and implementing a personal development plan, it is important to set yourself **goals**. For example, they could be linked to **physical** aspects of fitness, **technical** aspects of performance or aspects of strategy such as your **personal** qualities within a team.

These goals give you something to work towards and keep you focused while you try to improve your area for development. Goal setting can be important within any sportsperson's training plan because it acts as a motivational tool and helps the athlete to identify targets and monitor progress. There are, however, some difficulties with setting goals. Goal setting is often considered boring because it is usually time consuming, but it actually allows the athlete to dedicate more time to training in the long run. Finally, the athlete may set the wrong goals such as outcome goals. Outcome goals are solely based on outcome – that is, when we only compare our own performances to those of others, rather than considering our personal improvements.

TYPES OF GOALS

It's useful to define your goals, because these will influence your mindset and the way you approach an activity. There are three types of goals:

- Outcome goals
- Performance goals
- Processing goals

Outcome goals

Outcome goals focus on the **result.** You directly compare your own or your team's performance against other performances.

Performance goals

Performance goals focus on **personal performance**. Your performance is not compared to others. Achieving personal goals can result in performance satisfaction and, in turn, boost confidence.

Processing goals

Processing goals focus on **technique** rather than the result. Athletes who participate in sports that require a high level of precision often set processing goals.

 **ACTIVITY**

Below are examples of the types of goals that athletes might set themselves. Try filling in the blank boxes with your own examples.

	OUTCOME GOALS	PERFORMANCE GOALS	PROCESSING GOALS
Team activity	**Hockey** Before a hockey match, a team will be focused on scoring more goals than the opposition and, ultimately, winning the game.		**Football** A footballer might choose to practise their free kicks. During the practice, the footballer would focus on their technique – placing their foot next to the ball and getting a consistent ball strike.
Individual activity		**Cycling** Prior to a cycling race, an athlete might be more focused on their personal performance – for example, by achieving a personal best time – than on winning the race itself.	

SHORT- AND LONG-TERM GOALS

When goal setting, it is important that you have a clear idea of what you want to achieve. Teams and individual athletes usually set long-term goals by the end of the season or year. Likewise, at the start of your personal development plan you should have a clear idea of what you want to achieve by the end of your plan. To achieve these long-term goals, you need a series of short-term goals to help you to:

- remain focused throughout your period of training
- break the long-term goals up into more manageable chunks
- maintain steady improvement and, therefore, keep you motivated
- prevent boredom.

The 'staircase' model is often used to show how long- and short-term planning works. Have a look at the diagram below.

EXAMPLE   BADMINTON

This example illustrates the short-term goals that a badminton player might use to achieve their long-term goal of being selected for a regional squad.

		December — Finish
	November	Represent regional squad at national event
	October	Attend regional training camp
	September	Achieve selection for regional squad
	August	Win inter-schools tournament
July		Preparation phase – work on footwork and shot selection
Start		

EFFECTIVE GOAL SETTING: THE 'SMARTER' APPROACH

When you are preparing your personal development plan, you need to follow certain principles to ensure that you achieve your long- and short-term goals.

The acronym 'SMARTER' is often applied to goal setting.

Specific – Your goals should be clear and precise. They should reflect your ability and experience within your chosen activity.

Measurable – Set targets that can be tracked and monitored easily over time.

Agreed – Your goals need to be approved by a teacher or coach. This means you are fully supported by someone with experience and knowledge in your chosen activity.

Realistic – Realistic goals are more likely to be achieved and you are, therefore, more likely to stay motivated throughout your personal development plan. Setting unrealistic goals will result in lack of success and, ultimately, result in a drop in morale.

Timed-phased – Your goals should be progressive. Planning short-term goals will ensure ongoing progress and help you achieve your long-term goals.

Exciting – Make sure your goals are rewarding and enjoyable. This approach will maintain motivation and prevent you from becoming bored.

Recorded – Keep track of your performance. This allows comparisons from one week to the next, and allows for long-term monitoring of progress.

THINGS TO DO AND THINK ABOUT

1 Explain why goal setting is important either:
   a before the beginning of a season, or
   b when planning your personal development plan.

2 Choose one activity on your course and create a similar 'staircase' model to the one above. Fill in the short-term goals that will help you work towards your long-term goal.

3 Look back over your 'staircase' model and other goals that you might have set for activities on your course. Do the goals you set fulfil the 'SMARTER' criteria?

DON'T FORGET

Although goal setting might seem boring or time consuming at first, in the long run it saves time and allows for smarter training.

ONLINE

Head to www. brightredbooks.net/N5PE for a link to a useful website and apps for goal setting.

VIDEO LINK

Watch the video at www. brightredbooks.net/N5PE to help reinforce what you have learned. Listen carefully to how the hockey player thinks she will set short- and long-term goals.

ONLINE TEST

Test yourself on goal setting online at www. brightredbooks.net/N5PE

MONITORING TRAINING

It is imperative to monitor your training throughout the season by gathering data using appropriate methods specific to your activity. This allows you to check whether your personal development plan is effective or not, or whether changes need to be made.

TRAINING DIARY

A training diary is a very effective way of monitoring the plan because it allows the performer to consider aspects such as weather conditions, how they were feeling during the session on a scale of 1–10 or whether they found the session too difficult or too easy. The performer can refer back to the diary at a later date to compare or to make adaptations throughout the season. It provides the performer and the coach with invaluable information.

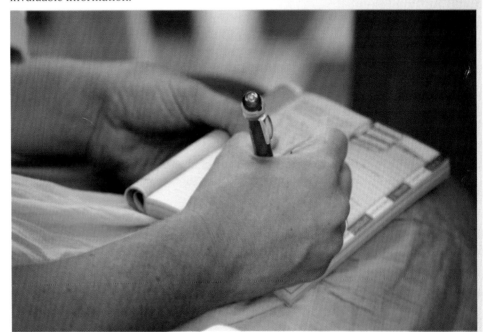

ONLINE

Downloading a training app can be a great way to monitor your performance - try out *Training Peaks* or *Vision Personal Training*.

ONLINE

My Workout Diary and *Map my Fitness* are other useful apps for training.

Another useful method of monitoring your training is by using a heart rate monitor. Several football teams have begun to use them to track how their players' hearts respond to certain types of training. Heart rate monitors can also help to identify whether a player is about to come down with a cold or fever. When this is the case, there is an increase in heart rate even if the body is at rest. This can, therefore, be identified without overexerting yourself.

EVALUATING

Another method that can be used to monitor your programme of work would be to repeat the methods you used to gather information at the start of your training and compare your results throughout your plan.

EXAMPLE TRAINING DIARY

Here is an example of a training diary

	Session 1	Session 2	Session 3	Session 4
WK 1 *Date:11.4.13*	Interval training 8 × 300 m Pace: 60 secs Rest: 60 secs Weather: blustery conditions on back straight. Difficulty: coped well with session, rest period could have been extended to 75 secs.	Continuous run 20 minutes Weather – heavy rain made conditions difficult. Difficulty: maintained steady pace throughout run. Covered 2.7 miles in 20 minutes.	Fartlek session Weather Difficulty:	
WK 2				
	After week 2, I will apply **progressive overload** to my training: • Increasing the **intensity** of my interval training • Increase the **duration** of continuous runs and Fartlek training • Re-test			
WK 3				
WK 4				
	After week 4, I will apply **progressive overload** to my training: • Increasing the **intensity** of my interval training • Increasing the **duration** of continuous runs and Fartlek training • Increasing the **frequency** of training sessions • Re-test			
WK 5				
WK 6				
	Re-test			

SUMMARY

The reasons for monitoring and evaluating your training are to:

- allow comparisons with previous information you have gathered
- check what progress you have made
- check if you've met your targets
- assess whether your personal development plan is appropriate
- assess whether you need to make changes/adaptations to your plan
- identify any new strengths/weaknesses
- motivate you to keep working or to work harder.

VIDEO LINK

Check out the 'Benefits of Heart Rate Training' videos at www.brightredbooks.net/N5PE

DON'T FORGET

You must monitor your training regularly to ensure that you are on track to reach your targets. If you don't, you might not reach your potential. Keeping a training diary up-to-date will enable you to plan ahead and adapt your training as and when required.

THINGS TO DO AND THINK ABOUT

1 What are some of the methods that you have used to monitor your training so far?

2 Why is it important to continually monitor your training throughout the season?

3 Do you think it would be helpful to use more than one method of monitoring your performance? If so, why?

ONLINE TEST

Take the 'Monitoring training' test online at www.brightredbooks.net/N5PE

TRAINING METHODS 1

There are a number of training methods you can use to develop a specific skill or refine a technique. These are explained in more detail below. The method(s) you adopt will depend on:

- your stage of learning
- the type of skill you are developing
- whether it's a simple or complex skill
- prior knowledge of the skill
- your ability level.

SOLO PRACTICE

Solo practice is commonly used when a performer is either learning a completely new skill for the first time or identifying the particular subroutine of the skill that they are having difficulty with.

EXAMPLE FOOTBALL

Football is a sport where some skills can be practised alone. When practising free kicks, you can use obstacles to simulate opposition. During solo practice, you could set yourself certain challenges that you try to achieve, or aim for certain areas of the goal from specific areas around the box. This type of practice allows you to isolate and practise skills with no distractions or pressure from external sources. However, one disadvantage is that you won't receive external feedback.

EXAMPLE TABLE TENNIS

Like a football player, a table tennis player could choose to practise serving on their own by setting up targets on the table, marking areas they would want to hit during their serve, or serving continuously and in different ways to try to perfect their action.

VIDEO LINK

Watch the 'Shadow Play' video at www.brightredbooks.net/N5PE

SHADOW PRACTICE

The concept of shadow practice is to watch another player's movement – preferably a model performer – and to mirror it. This type of practice is particularly useful for activities that involve 1 v. 1 competition, and those where you are required to match the opposition's movements.

EXAMPLE BASKETBALL

During a game of basketball, teams often select a man-to-man defence as their defensive structure. Man-to-man defence requires you to directly mark a member of the opposition team as they move around the court. You can use shadow practice to practise the same type of movement as that required in a man-to-man defensive structure. The practice would start with a player standing opposite you. Initially, the demands of the practice might be low (only moving forward, back or side to side). As your movement and shadowing improves, however, the player opposite might choose to move faster and in any direction. Finally, the player opposite might include a ball in the practice which will not only require you to shadow, but to concentrate on the basketball too.

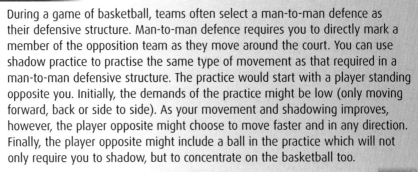

contd

EXAMPLE   BADMINTON

The use of shadow practice is particularly popular in badminton. This type of practice allows you to practise your foot work around the court and your repertoire of shots without the need to hit a shuttle. A practice might consist of you starting in the centre of the court in the 'ready position'. You move according to the player on the opposite side of the court, mirroring the shot they play and moving to the same area of the court they do. After each shot, both players return to the centre of the court in the 'ready position'.

PARTNER PRACTICE

Partner practice gives your practice sessions some variation, and allows you to work cooperatively with your partner to help you learn the skill in a more closed environment. Your partner can also offer valuable feedback because they are able to view your technique from a different perspective. As your skill level increases, your partner can introduce an element of competition to make the practice more challenging.

 DON'T FORGET

When you are training to improve a specific skill or technique, the methods of practice that you use will be appropriate to and dependent on the stage of learning that you are at.

EXAMPLE   BASKETBALL

The set and jump shot in basketball requires a lot of practice to be consistently successful. By using partner practice, you can make the practice fun and introduce an element of competition. For example, you could start off with your partner gathering rebounds and passing you the ball as you try to shoot from different parts of the court. Then, to increase competition, you and your partner could choose five different points on the court to shoot from: the first to score from all five points is the winner. Finally, your partner could inbound the ball from the base line and follow the ball out, trying to block your shot in the process. There is an element of pressure introduced at each different stage of this practice which should benefit your performance during games.

 ONLINE TEST

How much do you know about 'Training methods'? Test yourself online at www.brightredbooks.net/N5PE

 THINGS TO DO AND THINK ABOUT

Consider each form of focused practice. Can you give examples of times you have used them on your course?

TRAINING METHODS 2

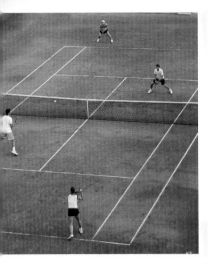

GROUP PRACTICE

You can progress from solo practice methods to group practice by introducing other players.

> **EXAMPLE** TENNIS
>
> In tennis, the inclusion of another two players introduces a further element of tactics and teamwork. Group practice allows you to practise movement, tactics and communication as part of a team. Group practice also gives you the opportunity to practise forehand and backhand shot routines that you might use during a doubles match.

OPPOSED/UNOPPOSED PRACTICE

When you are practising certain skills or rehearsing specific structures or strategies within your activity, it's useful to be able to alter the amount of pressure the opposition exerts on you. When you are just beginning to learn a skill or structure, too much pressure will result in you making mistakes and losing confidence. As your skill level increases, however, so too should the pressure from opposition. The amount of pressure usually depends on what **stage of learning** you are at. So, for example:

- practising with no opposition is usually done at the preparation stage
- practising with passive (limited) opposition is common at the practice stage
- practising with active opposition is common when a skill becomes automatic.

> **EXAMPLE** RUGBY DEFENCE
>
> Rugby novices usually learn skills in isolation because there is no pressure from the opposition and they have an opportunity to grasp the skills without the risk of injury. As they progress and their skills improve, teachers and coaches might introduce an element of pressure such as a 'touch' tackle. This allows players to get used to the pressure of opposition during a game, but again prevents the risk of injury. Once a player becomes experienced in rugby and their skills become 'second nature' or automatic, they can train and play with active opposition, which means that contact is involved.

GRADUAL BUILD-UP

Gradual build-up breaks a skill down into steps. Each successive step is designed to be more challenging, so that when all the steps are completed, the skill is learned. This method of training is particularly useful when you are learning a complex skill with many steps, or a skill that has an element of risk involved when you are performing it.

> **EXAMPLE** VAULTING: HANDSPRING
>
> A handspring in gymnastics is a complex skill with a number of different elements. It would be dangerous and unsafe for you to try and perform a handspring as a whole without learning the technique beforehand. Therefore, to make it safe and more manageable, the skill is broken down into stages. Over time, you will become more confident and competent at performing the stages leading up to a handspring, and you'll eventually be able to try the whole skill.

REPETITION PRACTICE

Repetition practice involves breaking a skill down into its component parts and practising the individual parts repeatedly. This practice can also involve repeating the whole technique. This type of practice is particularly popular with complex, closed skills that require the same technique to be reproduced a number of times. For example, a golf swing or a tennis serve require the same motion and movement pattern to be reproduced accurately. Repetition practice allows you to practice each part of the technique so that it moves seamlessly into the next.

THINGS TO DO AND THINK ABOUT

1 There are times when experienced teams use passive opposition during training. Can you think of why a team might use passive or no opposition instead of an active defence during training?

2 Give examples of activities where you have used opposed or unopposed practices. Explain why you used that type of opposition.

3 Can you explain times when you have used gradual build-up on your course?

4 Can you explain times when you have used repetition practice on your course?

DON'T FORGET

Skill-related training methods are different from the methods used to develop a physical or mental aspect of your performance. The methods that you use must be specific to the area that you want to improve and specific to the activity:
- Skill-related methods: solo, massed, shadow, repetition, continuous, pressure drills, conditioned games.
- Physical methods: interval, continuous, Fartlek, stretching, circuits.
- Mental methods: visualisation, breathing technique.

ONLINE TEST

How much do you know about 'Training methods'? Test yourself online at www.brightredbooks.net/N5PE

TRAINING METHODS 3

MASSED/DISTRIBUTED PRACTICE

Should you use massed (continuous) practice or distributed (spaced) practice? Before you decide, you need to consider the following:

- Whether the skill is complex or simple.
- The motivation and experience of the performer.
- The intensity of the activity.

Massed

EXAMPLE   ROWING

Rowing requires you to create a lot of power and maintain good technique, and this will inevitably fatigue you over time. Therefore, using massed practice is an effective way of training in a similar situation to that of an actual race.

Distributed

EXAMPLE   GYMNASTICS FLOOR WORK

Short, distributed practice is an effective way to rehearse a gymnastics floor routine, because it enables you to practise in short slots of time, which prevents fatigue and the risk of injury. You would aim to get as much quality out of your practice as possible during the short slots. During the rest periods, you could receive feedback on your performance as well as mentally rehearsing what you are going to do in your next short practice.

CONDITIONED/SMALL-SIDED/COACHED GAMES

When you first begin to develop a skill, it's useful to be able to practise it in a less pressurised, 'conditioned' environment where the rules are relaxed. Teachers and coaches often use this method to emphasise a specific skill, technique or teaching point. More experienced performers also use these training methods, but their aim is to increase the pressure on them rather than reduce it. This type of practice means that a player must adapt and learn to deal with high pressure situations, and can consequently cope better during games. This form of conditioned/small-sided games would only be used for performers in the **automatic** stage of learning.

contd

Conditioned games

> **EXAMPLE**   FOOTBALL
>
> **1. Passing**
> During football training a teacher or coach might want to emphasise the skill of passing along the ground. They could change the rules and impose the condition that the ball must stay on the ground at all times, forcing players to adapt and practise different passes along the ground to team mates.
>
> **2. Use of width**
> Likewise, a coach or teacher might section off a channel down each side of the pitch. They could change the rules so that the ball must be played out to these channels during an attack. This condition emphasises width in attack and the importance of pulling defenders wide to create space in the middle of the pitch.

Small-sided games

In small-sided games, the number of players in each team is reduced. This means that each player gets a better opportunity to develop their skills and techniques within a game setting. It is important that the demands mirror that of a competitive match and are aimed at the correct ability level of the performer.

Coached games

In coached games, your coach or teacher might stop the game to emphasise a specific teaching point, offer external feedback or highlight examples of good practice.

WHOLE-PART-WHOLE

To use this method effectively, you need to be able to demonstrate the whole activity, then break the skill down into its component parts and practise them in isolation. Once you have practised a specific part or parts, you put the skill back together again and perform it as a whole.

> **EXAMPLE**   SWIMMING: FRONT CRAWL
>
> The whole–part–whole training method is often used in swimming. First, you perform the whole stroke, then break the front crawl action down and concentrate on each part. For example, you could isolate your leg kick and practise that using a float. Or you could isolate arm action, push and glide or breathing action. Once you have developed each individual component, you go back and perform the whole stroke again with improvements in each area of the stroke.

 VIDEO LINK

Check out the video about attacking drills at www. brightredbooks.net/N5PE

 ONLINE TEST

How much do you know about 'Training methods'? Test yourself online at www. brightredbooks.net/N5PE

 THINGS TO DO AND THINK ABOUT

Can you give an example of when you used small-sided or conditioned games on your course?

a What were the conditions? How did the conditions change the game?

b Why were the numbers reduced? Did it help you learn the skill or technique better?

PRINCIPLES OF EFFECTIVE PRACTICE

Here are the seven Principles of Effective Practice:

Intensity of practice

Work/rest ratio

Achievable progressive stages

Strengths and weaknesses

Awareness of skilled performer

Clear objectives

Effect of boredom and fatigue

For practice to be effective it should:

- have clear and achievable objectives
- be specific to improving your skill and technique weakness
- avoid becoming repetitive – this will lead to boredom
- avoid overtraining – this can lead to fatigue and injury
- be based upon your existing level of ability.

INTENSITY OF PRACTICE

How intensely you practise specific drills is closely related to the work/rest ratio, how experienced you are and the stage of learning you are currently at. For example, if you are at the cognitive stage of learning and you want to improve your overhead clear in badminton, you must be given sufficient time to recover after each drill. If you aren't, you will become fatigued and you won't perform the shot well. You'll probably then become demotivated and begin to lose confidence. The intensity must therefore be challenging but achievable to encourage the performer to remain motivated to improve.

When you have reached the automatic stage of learning, you need to introduce pressure into your practices to get you used to the pressure you'll face during competitions, and to force you to adapt the skill and technique to a variety of situations. For example, in a team activity this could involve introducing/increasing pressure from defence, while in an individual activity, such as badminton, you might have to play a competitive training game against a peer of similar ability.

WORK/REST RATIO

Work/rest ratio is the amount of time you work compared to the amount of time you rest. For example, if a 400m runner was doing interval training with a work/rest ratio of 1:3 and they worked for 45 seconds, they would rest for 135 seconds. To gain the most out of training sessions the work/rest ratio needs to be tailored to suit your specific needs and abilities and is very much dependant on which stage of learning you are at.

Work/rest ratio during training will depend on:

- your previous experience
- your ability level in the activity
- the physical demands of the practice/activity
- the difficulty of the skill being practised.

ACHIEVABLE PROGRESSIVE STAGES

If you want to progress in any activity, you need to remember the following:

- Practices should be challenging yet achievable.
- High-quality practice for a short period of time is more effective than low-quality practice for a long period of time.
- Training should be varied – avoid repeating the same practice over and over, even if you want to work on a single skill.

STRENGTHS AND WEAKNESSES

You must also be aware of what your own strengths and weaknesses are within your performance, or you might end up focusing attention on the wrong aspects. Don't just focus on your weaknesses – if you don't keep practising your strengths, then they'll become significantly weaker. It's vital to incorporate both in your practice.

AWARENESS OF SKILLED PERFORMER

The use of a skilled or model performer allows you to continually compare yourself to someone who can actually perform the skill effectively and efficiently, and it provides you with a visual image to memorise. A model could be a real person or a video clip.

CLEAR OBJECTIVES

The setting of short-term and long-term goals will motivate you to train and to continue to improve. Short-term goals could be on a week-to-week basis, or they could be specific targets that you set yourself within every training session. Long-term goals could be aimed at specific competitions or targets that you have set yourself and that you have hoped to have achieved by the end of the season.

EFFECT OF FATIGUE AND BOREDOM

Drills and practices at the cognitive stage of learning must be basic but still have some degree of challenge or the performer will become bored. If the drills at the practice stage are too challenging, the performer will fatigue quickly, but if they are too easy then they will become bored. Finally, at the automatic stage of learning, the drills should be more game-like, to put more pressure on the performer.

Training times depend on the nature and demands of an activity, but usually activities that contain endurance aspects such as swimming and long distance running tend to have long training times. High-impact, explosive activities such as sprint training or throwing events tend to be a lot shorter.

ONLINE

The apps *Ubersense* and *Coach My Video* are both very useful downloads.

DON'T FORGET

You need to think about the Principles of Effective Practice when you are designing a personal development plan to develop or learn a skill. These are equally important to the stage of learning you are at, the methods of practice that you intend to use and how you intend to monitor and evaluate your progress.

ONLINE TEST

Test yourself on the 'Principles of Effective Practice' online at www.brightredbooks.net/N5PE

THINGS TO DO AND THINK ABOUT

1. What are the Principles of Effective Practice?

2. Give some examples of why it is important to consider the Principles of Effective Practice when you are trying to improve your personal performance.

3. Try to think of an example where considering the Principles of Effective Practice has helped to improve your performance.

STAGES OF LEARNING

The three stages of learning can also be referred to as:

- Cognitive or planning stage (preparation stage)
- **Associative** stage (practice stage)
- **Autonomous** stage (automatic stage)

PREPARATION STAGE

At this stage, you break the skill down and learn about it in stages. Although this stage is commonly associated with beginners, this isn't always the case. For example, when experienced synchronised swimmers learn a new routine, they will initially break it down and learn the different components (subroutines) separately.

During this stage, you are bound to make a lot of errors. As a result, you'll get lots of **external feedback** and encouragement from your coaches or teachers to keep you motivated and help you to make progress.

When you are at this stage, visual and verbal explanations are often used to highlight key points within the skill or technique. The use of a **model performer** is an effective way of demonstrating effective technique.

EXAMPLE   RUGBY SPIN PASS

These are the characteristics of the preparation stage when you are learning the technique of a rugby spin pass:

- Teacher/coach starts with a verbal and visual demonstration (inclusion of model performer).
- You learn the basic technique to the spin pass.
- You get used to what each hand must do during the spin pass.
- Your pass will lack control and may be weaker off one hand than the other.
- Your pass will not always go to the intended target.
- You will receive a lot of feedback from teacher/coach.

PRACTICE STAGE

During the practice stage, you will start to join subroutines together, develop the skill and slowly learn to perform the skill under pressure.

contd

The length and frequency of your training sessions will depend on:

- Aptitude
- Level of fitness
- Motivation
- Past experience
- Complexity of skill – simple skills will require less practice than more complex skills.

Practising the skill or technique effectively, and in the right environment, will reduce performance errors and improve fluency and accuracy of movements. At this stage, you will be able to rely more on **internal feedback**. External feedback will also still play a role, but will focus less on technique and more on how to progress the skill by practising in different settings and under varying pressure.

> **EXAMPLE**   RUGBY SPIN PASS
>
> These are the characteristics of the practice stage when you are developing the technique of a rugby spin pass:
> - The spin pass becomes more natural.
> - You have more control over the direction and strength of the pass.
> - You are able to execute the pass in more pressurised situations.
> - You will start to rely more on internal feedback.
> - Coach/teacher feedback will be less corrective and will concentrate more on using and adapting the pass in a variety of situations.

AUTOMATIC STAGE

By this stage, you will be able to execute the subroutines automatically – that is, you don't need to think about **how** to execute the skill. At the automatic stage, timing and accuracy are consistently performed to a high standard.

At this stage of learning, there will be a considerable decrease in mistakes made during practices and competitive situations. Internal feedback becomes the main source of feedback, with coaches and teachers having less input.

> **EXAMPLE**   RUGBY SPIN PASS
>
> These are the characteristics of the automatic stage when you have mastered the technique of a rugby spin pass:
> - Pass accuracy and control is consistently performed to a high level and almost always goes to the intended target.
> - You no longer need to think about basic technique.
> - You rely on internal feedback to evaluate your performance.

VIDEO LINK

For more, watch the video on rugby passing at www.brightredbooks.net/N5PE

ONLINE TEST

Test yourself on the stages of learning online at www.brightredbooks.net/N5PE

 THINGS TO DO AND THINK ABOUT

1   Consider all three stages of learning: preparation, practice and automatic in relation to one sports technique you use. What stage of learning are you currently at?

2   List the key characteristics of this stage.

3   Now that you have established your stage of learning, consider the methods of practice that will enable you to develop and improve. Give an example of one method that you plan to use, and one training session using this method.

PLANNING, PREPARATION AND EVALUATION 1

Your performance is worth 40% of your overall grade. However, the performance component also requires you to plan, prepare and evaluate your performance and this component is worth 20% of your overall grade. In this section we will investigate how to best plan, prepare and evaluate your performance.

PLANNING AND PREPARING: AN OVERVIEW

Planning and preparing for your one-off performance accounts for 10% of the overall mark. You will be required to:

(a) describe two personal challenges you need to plan and prepare for in order to carry out your performance
(b) explain why these challenges are relevant to your performance
(c) describe how you plan to prepare yourself to meet these challenges
(d) carry out an appropriate warm-up routine prior to the beginning of your performance.

EXAMPLES OF PLANNING AND PREPARATION

Over the next few pages, we will look at three examples of how different challenges could affect different activities at the planning and preparation stage.

EXAMPLE   1. RUGBY

(a)
- A challenge facing you as a rugby player might be that you have previously played against the opposition and have prior knowledge that your opposite number is bigger and stronger than you are.
- Another challenge facing you as a rugby player might be that your level of arousal before a game is too high, and therefore you get overexcited.

(b)
- Playing against a player bigger and stronger than you are has a huge impact on your performance. During a match it is your responsibility to defend and attack against that player. If a player is bigger and stronger than you are, it will be difficult to directly attack your opposite player and run hard at them. This will also be a challenge in defence when trying to compete against them in a tackle.
- Level of arousal is important in rugby, as being at the right level will allow you to perform with fluency and composure. However, if your level of arousal is too high, this will cause you to become overexcited, which could lead to poor decisions being made and may result in a number of errors during the match.

contd

(c)
- To meet the challenge of a player who is bigger and stronger than you, your team might devise a strategy to attack different spaces on the pitch, away from this opposition player. Moves such as a missed pass will mean the opposition player does not get a chance to tackle you, and stretches the defence wider, therefore, creating other spaces to penetrate. Personally, you might decide that when you get the ball you might pass or kick the ball to avoid taking contact and risk losing the ball.
- Similarly, in defence you might choose to close down the space between you and the opposition player quickly, therefore, putting them under pressure by not allowing them time and space.
- To control your level of arousal you might use different techniques to calm yourself down. On the way to a match you might listen to music that allows you to remain calm and remain focused. Closer to the match you might take a few minutes to use breathing techniques. Breathing techniques would help lower your heart rate and level of arousal to allow you to start the game with more control.

EXAMPLE 2. GYMNASTICS

(a)
- A challenge facing you as a gymnast might be that you have never performed a solo sequence in front of an audience. You might, therefore, feel nervous and unsure about how the audience might react.
- Another challenge might be that you have difficulty remembering your whole sequence of moves in your floor routine.

(b)
- Performing in front of an audience can be a daunting task, especially if you have no experience of doing this. Having this added pressure could cause fear or anxiety and could lead to mistakes in your performance.
- It is important that your sequence skills are linked together with control and fluency. If, during a performance, you forget certain parts of your sequence, it might look disorganised and will not flow well together. Also, being unsure about your routine could lead to you become anxious before a sequence, and in turn impact on your overall performance.

(c)
- To meet the challenge of performing in front of an audience, you can use certain techniques that will help you to stay calm. For example, you can use breathing techniques to help you lower your heart rate and relax before a performance. You can also use positive self-talk to help you reassure yourself before a performance.
- To meet the challenge of remembering a sequence, you could use mental rehearsal. This allows you to practise the routine over and over in your head, so that when it comes to the actual performance you feel ready, because you know the routine inside out. You might also use mental cues to help you remember your sequence. If you are performing to music, you might link a certain skill with a part of the music. Or, if you are not performing to music, you might remember the skills in sets of three to help you focus on the whole routine.

 DON'T FORGET

Every performer will face unique and individual challenges. Think hard about your own experiences before setting out your answers.

 ONLINE TEST

How well have you learned this topic? Head to www.brightredbooks.net/N5PE and take the 'Planning, preparation and evaluation for performance' test.

 THINGS TO DO AND THINK ABOUT

Consider the two examples above and try to write practice answers for how you would plan and prepare for your own one-off performance.

PLANNING, PREPARATION AND EVALUATION 2

EXAMPLES OF PLANNING AND PREPARATION (CONTINUED)

EXAMPLE   3. TENNIS

(a)

- A challenge facing you as a tennis player might be that you find it difficult to remain focused throughout long matches.
- Another challenge might be that you get easily frustrated with yourself when you make mistakes.

(b)

- Tennis matches can last different lengths of time. As the match progresses, it is important that you remain focused to ensure you continue to make the right decisions and execute the skills with control. If you lose focus towards the end of a long tennis match, this is going to have a huge impact on your performance and ultimately the outcome of the match.
- Getting frustrated usually has a very detrimental effect on your performance. Without the ability to channel frustration correctly, it tends to show in other areas of your performance – for example, you could become increasingly frustrated when you make repeated errors and this could also affect your decision-making and self-control. This could ultimately mean that the number of errors greatly increases in your performance or that you get frustrated with the umpire's decisions and lose your temper on court.

(c)

- You can use a variety of methods to meet the challenge of loss of focus during a match. Diet and amount of sleep can have a big impact on focus and concentration. Before your tennis match, it is important to get a good night's sleep. The meals on the day of your match should consist of carbohydrates and vitamins that will provide your body with energy throughout the tennis match. Before and during the match, techniques such as positive self-talk will help you to focus on the task in hand and ensure you continue to make the correct decisions on shots.
- You can use breathing techniques, visualisation and positive self-talk to meet the challenge of getting frustrated after making a mistake. Before you begin the tennis match, you could use visualisation to picture certain shots your opponent might play and how you would react to them. This means that during a game you feel ready for certain situations when/if they arise. If you make a mistake during a game and you feel yourself becoming frustrated, techniques such as positive self-talk or deep breathing can help calm you down and refocus your mind.

EXAMPLES OF THE WARM-UP

Warming up in preparation for an activity is vital. It helps you to:

- increase blood flow to muscles
- warm muscles up to avoid injury
- practise skills that you will be performing in your activity
- prepare mentally for your performance.

VIDEO LINK

Check out the example aerobic warm-up at www. brightredbooks.net/N5PE

contd

In most activities there are three main parts of a warm-up:

1   Aerobic warm-up

2   Stretching

3   Skill-related practice

Aerobic warm-up

This is usually light exercise such as jogging, swimming or cycling. The purpose of this part of the warm-up is to raise your heart rate and increase the blood flow around your body to the muscles.

Stretching

There are two types of stretching – static and dynamic.

Static stretching is done standing still and requires stretches to be held for a period of time.

Dynamic stretching is done on the move and usually involves carrying out a number of stretches at a time – for example, high knees. Dynamic stretching is often used when warming up for an activity as the movements tend to mirror that of the activity you are about to take part in – for example, high knees is similar to the running technique.

Skill-related practice

This involves practising the specific skills from your activity. For example, if you play basketball you would practise lay-ups. A skill-related warm-up helps you to practise skills you are about to perform.

At each stage of the warm-up, you should also be focusing mentally on the activity you are about to participate in. However, team talks are also involved in your mental preparation for a performance.

EVALUATING YOUR PERFORMANCE

Following your performance, you are required to carry out an evaluation that relates to the challenges you identified and prepared for. As with the planning and preparation section, this section is also worth 10% of your overall grade.

As part of the evaluation you will be required to:

- evaluate your performance in relation to the two challenges you highlighted in the planning and preparation section

- evaluate your overall performance.

You should mention the following:

- Whether you effectively planned and prepared for the challenges of your performance. If you feel you did not, what could you have done differently?

- How you feel you performed overall.

- Did you make good decisions? If not, did you try to change it next time? Did you try to make up for any bad decisions?

- What would you do next for future performances?

DON'T FORGET

Keeping a training diary will help you immensely when it comes to evaluating your performance!

THINGS TO DO AND THINK ABOUT

Use your practice answers from the Things to Do and Think About on p83 to devise a suitable warm-up routine to execute prior to your performance. Test it out and rework it as you see fit.

ONLINE TEST

How well have you learned this topic? Head to www.brightredbooks.net/N5PE and take the 'Planning, preparation and evaluation for performance' test.

PORTFOLIO

SECTION 1: SELECTING AND EXPLAINING

OVERVIEW

The portfolio is split into three outcomes and will make up 40% of your final grade.

Section 1

Outcome 1: Demonstrate knowledge and understanding of factors that impact on personal performance – **8 marks (20% of the portfolio mark)**

Section 2

Outcome 2: Develop personal performance in physical activities – **16 marks (40% of the portfolio mark)**

Section 3

Outcome 3: Evaluate the performance development process – **16 marks (40% of the portfolio mark)**

SECTION 1

In this section you need to select and explain, in detail, the impact of two factors on performance in two different physical activities.

The factors that can impact on performance are mental, emotional, physical and social. Take a look at the 'Table of factors that impact on performance' in Appendix 1 (pp92–3). to remind yourself of them all.

Identifying factors that impact on performance

The table below will help you to identify the factors that impact on your performance and to plan a particular course of action.

DON'T FORGET

Consider all factors!

What I want to know:	
Factor 1 Mental	Positive impact
	Negative impact
Factor 2 Emotional	Positive impact
	Negative impact
Factor 3 Social	Positive impact
	Negative impact
Factor 4 Physical	Positive impact
	Negative impact
After considering all the factors, the factors that impact on my performance are:	

contd

You could also use a 'cause and effect chart' to help you identify specific aspects of these factors and the effect they have on your performance. There's an example below.

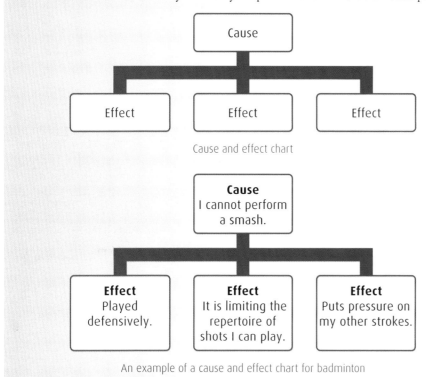

Cause and effect chart

An example of a cause and effect chart for badminton

 THINGS TO DO AND THINK ABOUT

Complete the table to examine more closely the factors that impact on your performance.

You should also try completing a cause and effect chart like the one above to identify the impact specific factors have on your performance.

 ONLINE TEST

Take the 'Section 1: selecting and explaining' test at www.brightredbooks.net/N5PE

SECTION 2: PLANNING, DEVELOPING AND IMPLEMENTING

OVERVIEW

You have identified the factors that impact on your performance in the previous section. You now need to focus on two of those factors in two different activities so you can develop and improve them. First, you need to choose appropriate methods of gathering information about the factors, and justify why you have chosen these methods. Then you need to gather the information. The table below illustrates some possible methods of gathering information.

METHODS OF GATHERING DATA/INFORMATION					
MENTAL	**EMOTIONAL**	**SOCIAL**	**PHYSICAL**		
• SCAT (Sport Competition Anxiety Test) • Questionnaires • Observation schedules • Self-reflection/self-profiling sheet • Personality inventory • Psychometric testing • Profile of mood status (POMS) • Bio feedback	• Disciplinary record • Questionnaire • Self-reflection • Coach feedback • Emotional intelligence quotient • Profile of mood status (POMS) • Bio feedback	• Questionnaire • Self-appraised • Team/group feedback • Coach feedback • Environmental checklist	**Fitness** • Standardised fitness tests • Time-related observation schedules • Digital analysis • Heart rate monitor • Static and dynamic testing	**Skills** • General observation schedule • Focused observation schedule • Scatter diagram • Digital analysis • Coach feedback • Skills testing • Field test	**Tactics/ composition** • Match analysis • Digital analysis • Coach feedback • Knowledge of results

THE 'DESCRIBE' QUESTION

When you are preparing your portfolio, you will be asked some 'describe' questions. These ask you to write about **how** you did something. Have a look at the following example and try to answer it:

(a) *Describe how you carried out your chosen method to gather information about the impact this factor had on your performance.*

(4 marks)

So you need to describe the following in detail:
- Your method of gathering information.
- Why you chose that method.
- How you used that method to gather information about the impact your chosen factor had on your performance.

PLANNING AN APPROPRIATE TRAINING PROGRAMME OF WORK

Once you have gathered sufficient data, you must plan an appropriate training programme of work to develop and improve the factor impacting on your performance. You must use the following tools and strategies:

- personal reflection sheet
- general performance sheet
- target/goal setting
- periodisation (refer to phases of training).

Preparing your plan

When you are preparing your plan, you must:
- gather information
- produce an annual plan (refer to periodisation and Principles of Training) including:
  – the major competitions over the year
  – school, district and national events
  – club or school fixtures.

You must identify the following areas on the plan:
- The aspect of your performance that you want to develop in each phase.
- The period of time that each phase will take up within the plan.
- The number of training sessions per week.
- The intensity of each weeks training sessions.
- Check points throughout the plan that allow you monitor training and progress.

contd

EXAMPLE

Impacting factor –Stamina	Monday	Tuesday	Wednesday	Thursday	Friday	Saturday	Sunday
Week 1	Session	Session	Session	Session	Session	Session	Session
	8x 200m Target time – 40 seconds Rest 120 seconds	Rest	Continuous run 20 minutes HR monitor used 65–85% max HR-Training zone	Rest	200m (race pace) 50m walk, 50m jog) × 10	22 minutes continuous run HR monitor 65–85% max per hour	Rest
Week 2	Session	Session	Session	Session	Session	Session	Session
	10x 200m Target time – 40 seconds Rest 120 seconds	Rest	Continuous run 22 minutes HR monitor used 65–85% max HR-Training zone	Rest	200m (race pace) 50m walk, 50m jog) × 10 Target 40 seconds	25 minutes continuous run. HR monitor 65–85% max per hour	Rest

 ACTIVITY

Create a snapshot programme of work that will develop and eventually improve the factor impacting on your performance. The programme should last between 6–8 weeks long. Have another look at the information in this section before you begin. You must show progression from week 1 to week 6 or 8.

THE 'EXPLAIN' QUESTION

When you are preparing your portfolio, you will also be asked some 'explain' questions. These ask you to write about **what** you did and **why** you did it. Have a look at the following example and try to answer it:

(b) Explain why you chose this method of gathering information on the specific impacting factor? *(4 marks)*

 DON'T FORGET

To answer a question that asks you to 'describe', you must write about how you did something.

DEVELOPING AN APPROPRIATE TRAINING PROGRAMME OF WORK

This table shows approaches you can use to develop your performance and how to build these into a programme of work.

 ONLINE TEST

Take the test on 'Section 2: planning, developing and implementing' at www.brightredbooks.net/N5PE

APPROACHES TO PERFORMANCE DEVELOPMENT					
MENTAL	**EMOTIONAL**	**SOCIAL**	**PHYSICAL**		
Development approaches *visualisation *relaxation techniques (deep breathing) *imagery *mental rehearsal *positive self-talk *cognitive and somatic techniques	*Development approaches* *team talks *rewards (intrinsic and extrinsic) *self-talk (3Rs —'recognise, regroup, refocus') *creative input *imagery *visualisation *mental rehearsal *conflict management techniques *assertiveness training *trust games *cognitive and somatic techniques (management of stress, emotions, and disappointment) *restorative practices	*Development approaches* *building team dynamics *partner/group work *use of role models *investigate access to neighbouring facilities *defining roles *peer groupings *national/local intervention programmes *community initiatives/trusts *national/local events *role models *plan to introduce a new activity *rebranding activities *self-esteem building activities *positive reinforcement techniques *active listening *process training *restorative practices	**Fitness** *Training approaches* *conditioning drills *Fartlek *interval *continuous *circuits *plyometrics *weight training *Principles of training* *specificity *progressive overload *frequency *intensity *duration *reversibility *adaptation *Phases of Training* *micro (preseason) training *macro (competition) training *miso (transition) training	**Skills** *Training approaches* *shadowing *repetition drills *pressure drills *conditioned games *combination drills *opposed and unopposed practices *gradual build-up *isolation drills/practices *massed and distributed practice *Principles of Effective Practice* *progression of practices *appreciation of work/rest ratio, *boredom *fatigue *consideration of strengths and weaknesses *comparison to model performer *variety *enjoyment *Goal setting* *SMART targets	**Tactical/compositional** *Training approaches* *opposed and unopposed practices *modifing or adapting strategies, formations and/or composition *pace of practice *walk/run-throughs/ rehearsal *technical sessions *theatrical techniques

SECTION 3: MONITORING, RECORDING AND EVALUATING

For the final part of your portfolio, you need to evaluate the performance development process by monitoring, recording and evaluating your performance development.

RECORDING

The method of recording you choose must be appropriate to the training you are doing.

> **EXAMPLE** MIDDLE DISTANCE RUNNER
>
> A middle distance runner has identified a poor level of stamina within his performance. This is having a negative impact on his performances over the season. He has decided to keep a training diary to help him monitor his training and progress. This includes the following:
> - a description of the training session, including work/rest ratio
> - targets/pace setting targets for the session
> - weather/surface
> - details of whether he has trained on his own or with training partners
> - how he has found the session: easy/difficult
> - whether he is fully fit or if he has picked up any injuries throughout the week.

By using this method of monitoring, the athlete is able to refer back to specific training sessions to identify what went particularly well or badly. He is also able to set personal pace targets relative to his target 1500m personal best. These short-term goals act as useful motivation tools to encourage the athlete to push himself on every training session. The goals set are also a good measure of how he is progressing from week to week.

> **EXAMPLE** FOOTBALL TEAM
>
> A football team identified that there was a distinct lack of width within their team. Although the structure that they were playing should have promoted width (4-4-2), the information that they gathered using a **match analysis grid** showed that the majority of the ball was played directly through the middle of the pitch with a very limited number of passes being made out wide. As a result of this information, the team implemented specific practices and conditioned games to encourage width. They completed another match analysis grid after weeks 1 & 2 and compared it to the initial match analysis grid. The improvement was clear: more passes were being made out to the right and left midfielders than before.

MONITORING AND EVALUATING TABLE

MONITORING AND EVALUATING					
MONITORING TOOLS					
MENTAL	**EMOTIONAL**	**SOCIAL**	**PHYSICAL**		
			Fitness	**Skills**	**Tactical/compositional**
*diary *SCAT *questionnaires *observation schedules self-reflection/self-profiling sheet *personality inventory *psychometric testing *profile of mood status (POMS) *bio feedback **Evaluation** *evaluative comparisons/statements	*diary *disciplinary record *questionnaire *coach feedback *self-reflection sheet **Evaluation** *evaluative comparisons/statements	*diary *questionnaire *self-appraisal *environmental checklist *team/group feedback *coach/teacher feedback *crowd/audience reaction **Evaluation** *evaluative comparisons/statements	*training diary *standardised fitness testing *static and dynamic testing *time-related observation schedule *digital analysis *pulse rate monitor **Evaluation** *evaluative comparisons/statements	*training diary *general observation schedule *focused observation schedule *scatter diagram *digital analysis *coach feedback *skills testing *field tests **Evaluation** *evaluative comparisons/statements	*training diary *knowledge of results *match analysis records *digital analysis *coach feedback *statistical analysis *score sheet **Evaluation** *evaluative comparisons/statements

 ## THINGS TO DO AND THINK ABOUT

Choose another factor which you now consider relevant for your continued performance development.

This factor must be different from the factors you explained in Section 1.

Have a look at the following example question and answer on monitoring and evaluating performance:

(a) Explain why it is necessary to monitor your performance development.   *(3marks)*

Monitoring performance is vital to improving performance. If you don't monitor your performance development throughout your training, it will be difficult to assess whether or not you've made any improvements.

Now have a go at answering the following questions. Some advice has been given with each question.

(b) Describe how you monitored your programme of work.

From the list in the table above, you are being asked to consider the methods you used to monitor your programme of work.

(c) Explain the decisions you made.

While you were carrying out your programme of work and monitoring it, you will have made decisions which you must now explain.

(d) Explain this factor.

You may draw on information you have gathered from monitoring and recording your performance development, any feedback you have received from others, or any self-evaluation you have carried out.

 DON'T FORGET

You need to focus on two factors in two different activities so you can develop and improve them.

 ONLINE TEST

Take the test 'Section 3: monitoring, recording and evaluating' at www.brightredbooks.net/N5PE

APPENDICES

APPENDIX 1

TABLE OF FACTORS THAT IMPACT ON PERFORMANCE

FACTORS THAT IMPACT ON PERFORMANCE		
MENTAL	**EMOTIONAL**	**SOCIAL**
Considerations: • concentration • level of arousal (under and over) • motivation • decision-making • problem-solving • attention span • focus of attention • mental toughness • processing information • anticipation • cue recognition • perception	**Main emotions:** ***Happiness/sadness*** (affecting confidence, and belief in self/own ability, resilience, optimism/ pessimism realising potential). ***Anger*** (affecting decision-making, self-control — controlling or channelling aggression, hostility, lowered tolerance of frustration) ***Fear*** (affecting decision-making, confidence, realising potential, panic, confusion, stress, anxiety, nervousness) ***Trust*** (affecting self-respect, mutual respect, personal responsibility, collective/team responsibility, adaptability) ***Surprise*** (affecting decision-making, confidence, resilience, determination)	**Group dynamics:** • cooperating/competing • contributing to team/group • working in isolation • relationship • role/responsibility for the performance • team dynamic **Cultural/societal issues:** • inclusion • gender issues • etiquette • respect for self and others • ethics • fair play • codes of conduct • conduct of self, players, crowd, and officials • social responsibility • role models • citizenship **Extrinsic motivation:** • prestige • money • media • sponsorship • fame • peer group pressure **Intrinsic motivation:** • empathy • self-esteem • initiative • self-discipline • offer, give and accept feedback or guidance • leadership **Environmental issues:** • barriers to participation (access to facilities, cost, location, seasonality of activity)

PHYSICAL

Fitness	Skills	Tactical/Compositional
Activity and role-related specific fitness requirements ***Aspects of physical fitness:*** • aerobic endurance/stamina • anaerobic endurance • speed endurance • flexibility/suppleness • strength • local muscular endurance • speed • power ***Aspects of skill related fitness:*** • agility • balance • control/core stability • reaction time/anticipation • coordination ***Physiology:*** • Body type (endomorph, mesomorph, ectomorph)	**Skill Repertoire** ***Skill classification:*** • simple/complex • open/closed • serial/discrete ***Technical qualities:*** • timing • rhythm • consistency ***Special qualities:*** • imagination • flair • creativity ***Quality of performance:*** • fluency • effort • accuracy • control ***Stages of learning:*** • cognitive • associative • automatic ***Information processing:*** • input • decision-making • output • feedback **Kinaesthetic awareness**	***Benefits and limitations of:*** • tactics • routines • compositional form ***Performance considerations:*** • personal strengths and weaknesses • role-related demands • team/group strengths and weaknesses • time of play • score • type of surface • opposition • previous history • environmental conditions ***Decision-making Principles of Play:*** • width • depth • mobility • penetration • support • communication • creativity • tempo ***Choreographic devices:*** • creativity, flair • mobility • tempo • perception • improvisation • repetition • variation (contrast, spatial patterns, levels, flow) • rhythm • expression

APPENDIX 2

PREPARATION, ACTION AND RECOVERY (PAR) SHEET

PHASE OF ACTION	Features of model performance SUBROUTINES	My Performance 1 Date:	My Performance 2 Date:
PREPARATION			
ACTION			
RECOVERY			

APPENDIX 3

COMPLETED MATCH ANALYSIS GRID

Here is an example of a match analysis grid that was completed while watching a videoed performance of a hockey match. Each tick (✔) corresponds to where the ball has been passed and received successfully in the different sections of the pitch. This identifies where the ball has predominantly been played. It also highlights where the areas of weaknesses are within the team's structure – this can be seen in the areas of the pitch which have little or no ticks (✔) in them.

✔ ✔ ✔	✔ ✔ ✔	✔ ✔ ✔ ✔ ✔ ✔
✔ ✔ ✔ ✔ ✔ ✔ ✔ ✔ ✔ ✔	✔ ✔	✔ ✔ ✔ ✔ ✔ ✔ ✔ ✔
✔ ✔	✔ ✔ ✔ ✔ ✔ ✔	✔ ✔

BLANK MATCH ANALYSIS GRID

agility
the ability to change the direction of the body in an efficient and effective manner

anger
if uncontrolled, can affect decision-making and can lead to loss of self-control

balance
the ability to retain the centre of gravity over the base of support. Balance requires the control of different muscle groups

codes of conduct
guidelines that outline acceptable standards of behaviour for you, other players, officials and the crowd

communication
the ability to impart and take on information

concentration
the ability to completely focus your attention on something for a period of time

control/core stability
the ability to move the body with confidence and steadiness

coordination
the ability to react quickly to stimuli

decision-making
the ability to make calculated decisions quickly

depth in attack
players are placed behind the attackers. If no forward movement is possible, therefore, play can be passed backward to the supporting players. This will provide cover and possibly create a new scoring opportunity

depth in defence
a second defender moves behind the defender who is pressuring the ball to support them if they're beaten

fear
can cause panic, stress, anxiety and nervousness, which affects decision-making, confidence and ability to realise potential

ectomorph
a predominantly ectomorphic individual is long, slender and thin, and power and strength sports are probably less suitable for them as their slight build leaves them susceptible to injuries. Their lack of musculature severely limits their chances in sports requiring mass. Ectomorphs dominate endurance sports and gymnastics

empathy
awareness of another's thoughts and feelings

endomorph
an individual who is pear-shaped and who carries excess body fat. Their mass hampers their ability to compete in sports requiring high levels of **agility** or **speed** and to perform sustained weight-bearing **aerobic** activities such as running

endurance
the ability to perform an activity for a long period of time. There are four basic types: aerobic, anaerobic, local muscular and speed endurance
aerobic endurance
the ability to transport sufficient oxygen to the working muscles during sustained exercise
anaerobic endurance
the ability to perform shorter, high-intensity exercises that don't rely on oxygen to be completed
local muscular endurance
the ability of a muscle or group of muscles to work continuously for a long time without tiring
speed endurance
the ability to prolong the amount of time where a near-maximum speed can be maintained

environmental factors
barriers to participation such as access to facilities, cost, location, travel, seasonality of activity

ethics
these are used to guide sportsmen and women, coaches and referees on how to conduct themselves in sports. They ensure that they meet the ethical standards in relationships, humanity, cooperation, commitment, safety and competence

etiquette
the expected code of behaviour from athletes in a particular sport

extrinsic motivation
factors from external sources such as money, prizes, acclaim, status and praise

flexibility/suppleness
the ability to move joints through a full range of motions

group dynamics
these include the following:
– cooperating whether it be with a coach, teacher or team mates
– contributing to team/group
– working in isolation
– relationships
– role/responsibility for the performance
– team dynamic

happiness/sadness
can affect confidence and self-belief, resilience, optimism/pessimism and ability to realise potential

information processing
the ability to separate essential and non-essential information during a performance

intrinsic motivation
a personal desire to succeed

kinaesthetic awareness
intrinsic or internal feedback from feelings in your muscles and joints and from your sense of balance as a direct result of carrying out a skill

level of arousal
your level of excitement and readiness to perform

mesomorph
a mesomorphic individual excels in strength, agility, and speed. Their medium structure and height, along with their tendency to gain muscle and strength easily makes them a strong candidate for a top athlete in any sport. They can sustain low body fat levels and find it easy to lose and gain weight

motivation
comes in two forms: extrinsic and intrinsic
extrinsic motivation
motivational factors such as money, lifestyle, status and fame
intrinsic motivation
a personal desire to achieve for the purpose of self-satisfaction

power
the combination of strength and speed

quality of performance
the ability to move with fluency, accuracy and control

reaction time/anticipation
the time between stimuli and muscular response

routines
a regular set of moves which makes up an action, practice or performance

skill classification
skills are classified into the following basic types:
simple skills
contain few, basic movements, which require few decisions to be made when they are executed
complex skills
require decisions to be made and a movement pattern to be selected from a range of possible choices. The movement pattern usually contains a number of difficult or complex movements to be carried out for the skill to be successful
open skills
the performer is not in control of all the factors that affect the execution of the skill

closed skills
the performer is in control of all the factors that affect the execution of the skill
serial skills
a group of discrete skills strung together to make a new and complex movement – for example, the sequence of movements for the triple jump
continuous skills
continuous skills have no obvious beginning or end and are repetitive
discrete skills
skills that have an obvious beginning and end

special qualities
these are qualities such as imagination, flair and creativity

speed
the ability to move the body and/or its parts quickly. For the body to move at speed, both arms and legs must move in an energy-efficient way

stages of learning
there are three stages of learning – cognitive, associative and automatic:
cognitive
this is where you learn a new skill. You are reliant on external feedback due to lack of experience
associative
this is where you perform the skill repeatedly. External and internal feedback are both required at this stage
automatic
this is where performing the skill becomes automatic and errors are more obvious. You can self-correct mistakes and focus more on other areas of your performance. Internal feedback is the main form used at this stage

strength
the ability to exert a force on an object while the muscles contract. There are three main types: dynamic strength, explosive strength and static strength

support
when players make themselves available to team mates in order to back up a particular move or action

surprise
affects decision-making, confidence, resilience and determination

tactics
a plan you make before you start playing in a game that takes into account your own or your opponents' strengths and weaknesses

technical qualities
these include timing, rhythm and consistency:
timing
the ability to perform a skill/action or movement at exactly the right time within a performance
rhythm
an activity or form of body movement that is based on a steady and prominent beat
consistency
the ability to do the same thing over and over again

tempo
the speed at which the game is played

timing
the ability to perform a skill/action or movement at exactly the right time within a performance

trust
affects self-respect, mutual respect, personal responsibility, collective/team responsibility and adaptability

width in attack
by placing attacking players across the width of the pitch, this will cause the opponents defenders to space out and, therefore, create more space to attack

width in defence
this is when you spread your defenders across the width of the pitch to effectively cover all areas of the pitch when your opponents have possession